The World
Saved by Kids

AND OTHER EPICS

T0268053

THE ITALIAN LIST

The World Saved by Kids

AND OTHER EPICS

Elsa Morante

Translated by Cristina Viti

LONDON NEW YORK CALCUTTA

Questo libro è stato tradotto grazie ad un contributo alla traduzione assegnato dal Ministero degli
Affari Esteri e della Cooperazione Internazionale Italiano

This book has been translated thanks to a contribution to the translation given by the Ministry of Foreign Affairs and International Cooperation of Italy

The Italian List
SERIES EDITOR: ALBERTO TOSCANO

Seagull Books, 2022

English translation © Cristina Viti, 2016

First published in English by Seagull Books, 2016

ISBN 978 1 8030 9 192 1

British Library Cataloguing-in-Publication Data

A catalogue record for this book is available
from the British Library

Typeset by Seagull Books, Calcutta, India
Printed and bound by WordsWorth India, New Delhi, India

Contents

Translator's Acknowledgements

This translation was greatly advanced by the ability to work closely on Elsa Morante's manuscripts at the Biblioteca Centrale Nazionale in Rome during a fruitful and enjoyable two-week stay at the Casa delle Traduzioni. Special thanks to Giuliana Zagra, Eleonora Cardinale and Francesca Amendola for their warm interest in my work, and to Maria Delfina Lanzavecchia, Simona Cives and Federica Quattrone for their kindness and hospitality.

Heartfelt thanks to Stephen Watts and Gareth Evans for understanding and encouraging my belief in this book, and to Alberto Toscano and everyone at Seagull Books for their editorial and typesetting inputs.

I am also grateful to the Estate of Elsa Morante for the courtesy with which my enquiries were met; to David and Helen Constantine, Tony Frazer and Aditi Machado for publishing sections of the book in *Modern Poetry in Translation*, *Shearsman Magazine* and *Asymptote* respectively; to Carlo Cecchi for lending his voice to the recording of *La sera domenicale* posted on the *Asymptote* website; and to Khayke Beruriah Wiegand for her advice on Hebrew-English transliteration.

My deepest, most tender thank you goes to my son Ryan, whose presence, conversation and technical support during work on this translation were a constant source of joy and inspiration, and whose sudden death cannot ever obscure the light he brought to all who knew him. This book, with all my love, I dedicate to his memory.

Foreword

For all those who want at all costs to know what 'literary genre' this book may belong to, the only possible reply is:

It is a romance of love and adventure (regularly divided into parts and chapters in which the main characters reappear under different guises).

It is an epic-heroic-lyrical-didactic poem in regular and irregular, free and rhymed verse.

It is an autobiography. It is a memorial. It is a manifesto. It is a ballet. It is a tragedy. It is a madrigal. It is a documentary in colour. It is a comic strip. It is a magic key.

It is a philosophico-social system (naturally involved with contemporary current affairs dominated by atomic idols and by the human conflicts between the first, second and third world; to which is added the memory of the other world—a memory that contemporary

philosophers routinely banish from conscious-
ness).

Etc. Etc. Etc.

In short, it is a book, if by book we mean a com-
mon and unique experience fulfilling a cycle
(from birth to death and vice versa). But if by
book we mean a product of a different sort, then
this is not a book.

So wrote Elsa Morante by way of a cover note for the
first edition of *Il mondo salvato dai ragazzini* in 1968—
an openly polemical but also, it seems to me, entirely
accurate description of the book, which she chose to
expand upon in her introduction to the 1971 edition.
On that and other occasions, she wrote of the poet as
a 'sensitive centre' continually returning to others
the value of reality and the hidden integrity of all
things by honouring the calling of the seeker/seer
and speaking out against the tragic farce of human
cruelty. Thus her manifesto ('a political manifesto
written with the grace of a fairy tale', as Pasolini put
it) extends the Sophoclean *es pantas auda* into an
exhortation for the poet to step into the public arena
as a fearless advocate of intelligent compassion. Her
memorial is dedicated, in the form of the astonishing
elegy that opens the book, to the young American
painter Bill Morrow, whose tragic death marked a
turning point in her life—but also to an ideal 'band
of brothers', the constellation of tutelary Happy Few
symbolically inscribed in a cross pattern, and by

extension to the 'kids' . . . no matter their age, who lost their life to bourgeois intolerance and State brutality. Her madrigal and her tragedy are choral polyphonies dynamically revisiting tradition by drawing upon and expanding established forms. Her magic key subtly encodes references to the more specific aspects of her *dérèglement raisonné*, while her comic strip incorporates deliberately facile rhyming, bombastic language, musical scores and layout alterations to expose and subvert the stupefying narrative of the media circus represented by the 'Great Masterwork'. But perhaps most importantly, her 'autobiography' and her 'novel' are, as she reminds us, not sequences of particular or personal facts but, rather, 'the desperate adventure of a consciousness that tends, in its workings, to identify itself with all other beings living on earth.'

Morante meets the rigorous demands of her poetic conscience by crafting a richly textured language infused with high, finely balanced energy. Reader and translator alike are implicitly invited to abandon any residual notion of words placidly 'ferried across' and move instead with the runaway rhythms, blasts of noise, exactingly poised musics and deep contemplative spaces of a strange and revitalizing journey. The end-notes supplied might provide some indications as to its 'lunatic route' while also shedding light on some of its perils and a few of its timeless landmarks.

Cristina Viti
Spring 2016

PART ONE
Farewell

I

Day after day the howl of the morning
tears me from the moonless place of your silence.
O heavenly night without resurrection
forgive me if once again I return to these voices.

I press my ear to the ground
to an absurd echo of the buried beats.
Chasing the fleeing unattainable beast
I throw myself onto the scent of blood.

I want to save you from the slaughter steals you
and take you back to sleep in your little bed.
But ashamed of your wounds you conceal
the pathways that lead to your lair.

I sham and laugh in a desperate dance
to distract you from the horrifying gloom

but your eyes discoloured under their eyelids
no longer wink at my love tricks.

Searching for your colours for your smile
I course the cities along a fading track.
Each boy walking by is a mirage.
I think I recognize you, for a moment.

And begging I run after a flickering curl
or a red T-shirt flitting round a corner . . .
But holed up in your cold hideaway
you despise my pitiful comedy.

A useless jester I rave roaming the streets
where every living breath denies you.
Then, at sundown, upturn on the desolate threshold
a game-bag full of bloodied feathers.

And I ask of the room's darkness some tenderness,
at least some decaying of memory,
senility, the misconstruction of vulgar time
that *heals all sorrows* . . .

But your death increases by the day.
And in this mounting spate I fall and rush back up
in a reckless race, for some sign,
some pointer in your direction.

O beloved unattainable nest,
there is no earthly step leads me to you.
Perhaps outside days and outside places?
Your death is the voice of a siren.

Perhaps through some perdition? or some grace?
or in what poison? in what drug?
perhaps in reason? or perhaps in sleep?
Your death is the voice of a siren.

Lust for a sleep that feels like some sweetness from you
but was the very imposture where I lost you!
Your death is the voice of a siren
who would waylay me into her pits away from you.

Perhaps, I have to accept every field rule:
each single degradation, each single patience.
I cannot jump over this barbed-wire mesh
while your innocent cry goes unanswered.

Your death is a blinding light in the night
it is an obscene laugh in the morning sky.
I am sentenced to time and to places
until the scandal is consummated over me.

Right here, I have to scheme and bargain with the beast
to rob it of the secret of my treasure.
O restraint of a slain childhood,
forgive me this indecency of surviving.

II

You left thinking you were playing the runaway.
Courting the spotlight with your farewell grimace.
Same old story! To then banish yourself to your cubbyhole
menacing behind your barred-up doors
like a great captain in his ultimate fort.
Woe on the audacious one should dare a siege!
But I know you. If nobody will dare
you'll tear yourself apart, and weep in childish anger
because there's no love in the world and you're forsaken.

But this time your door was slammed by hurricanes.
The rains rushed through the abandoned place
and a blood-like silt spattered the walls.
When you were alive, your room was the neighbourhood star,
sought after by all. And now
everyone shuns it, as if it were plague-stricken.
My foot stumbles on your poor vest
that no one's bothered to pick up from the floor.

On the balcony
laid waste by the winters, your plants have died.

Even thieves have sniffed at your ultimate fief
where indeed there was precious little to steal!
Cut out from magazines, your heroes' portraits
still adorn the walls: Gautama the Sublime,
bearded Fidel, suicide Billie Holiday.
Your cat's bowl is still sitting in a corner.
A thin red necktie hangs in the closet.

You left saddling yourself with your main possessions:
the cat in her basket and the briefcase phonograph.
'The rest of the luggage, ship it to me by sea.'
Three hundred times that ship has crossed that sea
and your treasures lie scattered, and I am here, alive.
Should I live three thousand years, course every sea,
I can no longer reach you to bring you back.

I know you thought you were playing farewell.
It was bravado, that grimace of yours . . .
But against the reckless wager of a boy
the stake at play is another drawn-out agony.

The thief of nights is a blind and deranged camel,
she roams bewitched Saharas, outside all tracks.
The route is lunatic, there is no destination.
The sands undo the traces of her thieving.

Her white eyes make mirages grow
from the torn bodies she sows across the sands.

And the mirages shift into multiplied distances
unattainable within their lonely fields.

Amputated off their bodies, they scatter, irredeemably
separate, eternal mutilations.
No mirage can meet another mirage.
Only solitudes are left, after the theft of bodies.

No addresses out there, nor any names, nor hours.
No sign for mutual recognition. The whole of eternal
                                        infinity
is but an empty white sky, sleepwalking wheel
where one flees blindly absent from the other.

The only chance to meet had been
this poor terrestrial point.

Over here the trouble kids, torn apart by an afternoon of
                                soul-rending anguish,
can still laugh at some silly joke.
Or in the boring neighbourhood, one boring Sunday,
be transfigured at a stroke on seeing a feather
and rush to paint a portrait of it, a magnified tragedy of
                                        colours
that pushes the blood of adult grief to burst its banks
into the childish firmaments.

Over here on an early autumn day, on a bridge that's
                                quivering with crowds
because of the Pope's passage,

you can show off, throwing yourself fully clothed into the
                                                        Tiber
to save a poor mongrel kitten
—the elect.
And climb back onto the bridge in a triumph, dripping
                                        and radiant.
But later on, back home, curse life
because that kitten refuses all food, and by now
just won't recover.

Over here, on a night of too much drinking, the roaring
                                                        kids
can get back home and in a frenzy of wild fun unleash
the jazz band on their record player, kick
furniture out of the way for a dance floor, throw open
the window screaming out unspeakable glorias and
                                        hosannas,
and when the Colonel complains from next door yell back:
                                        Fuck Off!
to then, in the morning, superciliously answer his further
                                        complaints with:
'A disgraceful rumpus?! in my apartment?!
Not even the cat stirred last night, in my house.
I think the only damn explanation, COLONEL,
is you must have had some nightmare last night—perhaps
a drop too much to drink?'

Over here you can swap life stories:
the brutal philistine father. The mistreated and beautiful
                                        mother

(aged three you'd defend her, shouting: 'This woman is
mine!').
The Cool Gran, fat and jolly and sick in her bones
(who had four husbands, and aged seventy-three
still made love to her fourth one the fiercest).
The Square Gran, shrunken and spry, who judges and
badmouths
and prefers solid jobs to any Art in the world ...
The first of November, with the pumpkin lanterns:
Treat-or-trick! Trick-or-treat!
And when, in competition with the blackbird,
you launched yourself from the garage roof
for a test flight ...

Over here, if a friend's far away, you can call him on the
phone,
never mind if he's at the antipodes (you don't have to pay
now anyway,
the bill is a future pluperfect): 'Who goes there?
Samarkand? London? Persepolis?
It's you!? It's me, from New York City!! Can you hear my
voice?
How are you? Dead boring here! Over there too? When
will you be back?
Hey! The cat sends her love, she's here
sat on my belly! Can you hear her voice? ...'

Over here you can cry for love betrayed.

You can whisper a deadly sentence into an ear
while sweetly kissing

that ear, laughing
childishly.

You can get locked up overnight and once released in the
                                                    morning
go down to the beach to cool off in the sea
thrashing and splashing and cursing
jailhouse fleas
and all stinking Codes and proclaiming the glory of being
an outlaw.

You can level your indignation at those vile lowbrow rags
that for filthy lucre insult the memory of Poets
with biographical gossip.
And, worriedly, intending to safeguard
yourself from any damn chance of future fame,
make sure you destroy there and then
your whole private correspondence.
Without even saving the original
snapshot (treasured since childhood)
of the Divine Old Big Ass Big Mama,
with her personal autographed dedication:
Thank you for the lovely New Year wishes.
Sincerely,
Mae West.

On summer mornings, you can go to the Via Appia,
and with your shirt off, under a battered straw hat,
paint an ancient sepulchre, that in your painting
                                                    becomes

a volcanic cliff, a savage petrified farewell
in the diluvial sky of Golgothas and Edens.
And as you paint, angrily dispute
because you are being contradicted when you state
that Cecilia Metella was a Catholic saint
the patroness of all Italian musicians
who, with a harp, appeared in a vision to the famous
                                        Italian musician
Giuseppe Verdi
the author of Tosca.

Over here, walking out of an upmarket florist's
in the company of your hysterical old mother,
you can grumpily offer her, inside a crumpled newspaper,
the hidden surprise and homage
of TWO DOZEN ORCHIDS! a dexterous theft
accomplished while the bourgeois florist was fawning
over the said lady.

On the first of November, the general feast
of All Saints,
with millionaire good cheer you can grandly
buy a whole turkey as a present for your cat
so she too can duly enjoy her name day
—for indeed she is called
Konkuahat.
And then, as you quarter the turkey, seized by a bitter
                                        disgust
for all animal deaths and all life,
feel like dying.

And with the same knife hack away at your wrist veins
in a solitary pitiful fit of mournful weeping
while the cat fills her face in the next room.

Over here you can spend whole hours listening to fairy
                                                              tales,
and enthusiastically read *Tropic of Cancer*.

You can insult a police station guard as you pass by
and get away with it, whistling, as if it had been
someone else.

You can idolize a great diva for years, and when at last
he deigns to be pleased to meet you
answer his formal politeness with nothing but: 'You bastard!'
and dump him in his Grand Hotel halls
shaking his dust from your boots.

You can take the ferry to the islands you didn't think
                                                       really existed
when you were a small child in Kentucky—but they do.
And once there radiantly dive head first into the sea from
                                                            the cliffs
racing on the heavenly crossing like an archangel in the
                                                        beating of wings;
or restfully let yourself be carried by the calm sea
on your little blue rubber lilo
getting tanned in the sun, cooled by the breath of the water,
like Unis the sultan (*lord of wisdom whose name his mother
                                                                ignores*)
lying between the palm-leaf fans

of his thirty thousand slave girls
along the Nile.

Over here you can seize the barbaric sunflowers
by leaping over the walls of private property.

You can write every other day to the cool gran
who when you were little would welcome you
to sleep next to her in her wide den
(when at night you were scared of winter witches
riding inside whirlwinds and hurricanes
astride bell towers ripped away from their churches).
And in the evenings you can share your bed with a
                                        friendly boy,
or with a girl, according to moods.
Or when you don't feel like lying down with anyone
because tonight you've lost hope and you want to be dead,
you can take the druggy pills that will have you
sleep like the dead till tomorrow.

Over here you can dance with a pretty girl you don't care
                                              for
so the ugly one you do care for will get jealous . . .

You can rescue a mangy little pye-dog from the gas chamber
and call him Prince Divinecountenance . . .

You can eat cannelloni, tiger prawns and vanilla ice
                                        cream . . .

You can, when you're too much of a beaut,
spit wrathfully at passers-by be they male or female

who presume to turn round in the street and follow you
                                      with their love-struck eyes.
And to get rid of them once and for all (I don't want to be
                                      liked!)
go out one day, with surly determination,
in your ugly-mug get-up (old-Jew specs, scarf up to your
                                      nose)
slipping darkly through the streets
looking like some highly wanted subversive dynamiter.

Over here you can discuss Christ and Buddha
and the Western ignominy we call middle class
and the Cuban revolution
and the whites, full of money, well-meaning & well-
                                      scrubbed, who stink of cesspit
and the poor blacks who have the scent of flowers
and the filthy wars of the fathers, their squalid peace
                                      treaties
and their institutions speculations missions inventions
                                      provisions & sanctions
all utter bullshit.
And reality, and pure sight, and UNDERSTANDING,
and multiple dimensions
and colours
and death.

Over here the kids laid waste by a frightening sickness
can, on awakening from an attack,
smile, calmed in their heavenly stupor
at an adoring face watching over them
even if then, forehead under the pillow, they'll hide

and say in a grief-stricken voice: 'So now
you know! You've seen me! And you expect me to believe
you can still bear with me . . . ?'

Over here; after screaming out during an insomnia 'I
want life
to cut loose from me!', having turned all the lamps in the
room
back on again, the boys can console themselves
saying to their girls as they look into the mirror together:
'See what a lovely couple we make, next to each other . . . '

Over here, bloodied from a street fight, the beaten boys
can take it out on their mothers back home, shouting at
them
for being found sat up waiting
like ambushing cops or like spies.
And the mothers shout back. But then, spotting
the shiner, they promise
for tomorrow a pair of dark glasses,
the best in the top designer outlet,
real tortoiseshell even:
and what's more a watch with the wheel
of universal time zones engraved all around it,
all solid Gold, guaranteed! no, make it
Platinum! . . .

And now here alone in this wake of ages
sitting in a corner of the room by the door
behind the window lit up in the night

I wait for the time of your return home.
I cannot give myself up to sleep, while you delay.
I want to have you back next to me, feel your breath
and cleanse you from the impossible leprosy
that has disfigured the laughter in your eyes.

I spy through the glass panes, listen out. In the distance
the bleak noise of the streets flows on like a toothed strip.
All the cities on earth are one goddamned gang in cahoots
against the heavenly kids.

The sleazy barflies, the vicious queens,
the ugly toxic rooms of cigarettes
the deafening basements
the demented homicidal fists
the cop chases
the traffics
the warped signals
the gardens of vampires
the wards of hospitals in delirium
the film stars the dolls the fairies the ambassadors
                              the middlemen the hired killers
the little baroque palazzos the skyscrapers
the urinals
the slimy stairs of bridges the river shacks
and railway tracks . . .
Latest Evening News
'With a blood-curdling scream'.
Without respite I pace from door to window.
I listen out for every step in the street.

And the long night advances. The rustle of wheels along
the tarmacs
grows less frequent. The shop signs go out.

The last lit-up windows are shut.
No more steps on the pavements.
No more gates screeching. An end to every late shudder
of the lift, its hoarse cogs rattling past each floor.

Until in the fading of the silent hour
a slumber bends my eyelids. My forehead crashes down
almost slamming onto the tabletop
in the tangled mess of my white hair.

And so, like in love endings . . .

And so I didn't hear your step, nor the clinking
of the little bunch of keys, nor the door opening
as you come home. Two childish hands
are tickling my nape.

I recognize, near my face, the nest-like flavour
of your hair. With my uncertain gaze I can make out
the luminous shadows of your eyes, the colour of a starlit sea.
'You hoodlum—is this the time? Here you are at last!

You might have told me, last night, you'd be out for the night!
What've you been up to? Something happen to you? some
fight? who crossed you?
Or some sickness . . . they got you drinking—again! did
you fall over? . . .

did you get hurt? where does it hurt?' . . .

'I am not hurt. I'm not in any pain.
Look at me, I'm well. Look, my body is intact.
But you—how old you've grown! you've gone and shrunk
                                                    on me!
Your hair's all white! your *lashes* are white!

When you smile, your face puckers up even more!
Poor cute funny little old lady.
I've come to say goodnight.
This is the hour of healing.

The hideous savage sickness hollowing us both
will end here. For all of my cruelties
I ask your forgiveness. And I too forgive you your
cruelty.

You knew that earthly childhoods
are a passage of divine barbarians
bearing the jailhouse mark of the ordained end.
You knew that. And yet you'd have me live
when I would no longer live.
Your forcefulness was a hassle for me.

The old, if they rejoice in a kid's presence,
see but fun and games in him. See nothing else.
You worshipped as a feast of your own destiny
a marked childhood that spoke its sickness to you.

Mirthful with the childhood I brought to you
you forgot the monotonous law that embroiders
its spectral patterns with an automaton's hand.
Your carefree ways were an insult to me.

Denying nature that had sentenced me from the start,
you would not understand me! To save
your only happiness and gratitude
you waved your fibs around like amulets.

When the spirits of slaughter threw me down with a
                                                                     howl
you stroked me where I'd fallen and said it was nothing.
When my eyes, aware and full of fear
asked you for help, you kissed them with a laugh.

You distracted me from insomnia with your fables
and listened to my dreams' desperate prophecies as if
they were fairy tales. You promised me I'd become
a king on earth, while earth was banishing me.

But I knew I was a cornered bandit.
To leave the game as a winner, laughing in the hangman's
                                                                     face,
I had nothing but another violence: my own, and precocious,
free with the last hooray!—and you fought me for it.

And so, through the meanness of your happiness,
you shopped me to the obtuse slaughter police
for the routine degradation procedure:
jailhouse, ugliness, decay.

And then, perhaps, once I was ugly, ruined, you too
                                                          would have banished me.
You are too childish! and mad! I know you!
I have always known you. That's why I am smiling at you
and have come to say goodbye. You are all my heart.

Even if I'm a mirage
don't be afraid of the daylight that might steal me from you.
Tonight, very soon, you too will be made a mirage.
The day has no more time to catch you by surprise.

Even if my name is delirium,
rest in this smile of my goodnight.
Only at this ultimate point could you still meet me.
This is our farewell.'

The thief of nights is a demented maniac
she hides each theft always in a different hole.
There is never a way out of those segregations.
No corridor or courtyard for those endless houses of
reclusion.
No common wall between one cell and the next.

The fantastic distance separating them
brooks no measure. No message is possible.
The rooms doorless: no windows, no top lights.
No post or alphabets or telephones or cypher books.

No pass you can cross through those ruinous
hungering dunes. No body of water for ships.
No body of air for voices.

But when memory is chewed up by the sands
even the pulsing of grief is cut short.

So be it.

PART TWO
The Chemical Comedy

I

My Pretty Postcard from Paradise

I had my passport, with the official visa from the
                    World Academy of Superior Chemistry
signed by Doctor & Shaman Laureates.
But the first armed guard I found in front of the
                    barred-up delta of the Bardo
was a murdered Aztec king
who yelled at me:
'No passengers here, except stowaways or illegal
                    expatriates. Get back!'
For which reason I did not cross the boundaries of
                    no man's land. Of kingdom come
all I could hardly see in the distance
was a transparent vault, hanging inside a quiet
                    amniotic twilight and adorned,
or so it seemed, with cheerful comic strips drawn
                    by an infant.
While far below me, in the shallows, I could still see
                    the body I'd just left

and it was turning to dust already, the skeleton
                              reduced to the bare breastbone
sending forth a faint glow, like a little gold belt . . .
The novelty of weightlessness got me high like the
                              first drinking spree at fifteen
when organs tissues veins all the pathways and
                              channels of circulation
are intact and clean in their wholesome freshness
so that alcohol rains ready & blessed like equinox
                              pollen into the centre of the flower.
Paradises! paradises! Nonetheless, relentlessly
                              enduring inside me
at the point of the solar nerve node like an abscess
                              with its pangs, was the certain news
that this Assumption was a provisional oneiric
        surrogate, like some quickie picked up on the
                              cheap
and that down below in the earthly station my next
        repatriation was already officially ordained.

II
Late Sunday Dusk

For the suffering of sick wards
and of all jailhouse walls
and of barbed-wire camps, hard-labour convicts &
                                    their guards,
and of ovens & Siberias & abattoirs
and of marches & solitudes & poisonings & suicides
and the shudders of conception
and the sugary taste of seed & of deaths,
for the numberless body of suffering
theirs and mine,
today I reject reason, majesty
denying the ultimate grace,
and choose to spend my Sunday with derangement.
O pierced prayer of elevation,
I claim for myself the guilt of the injury
in the base body.
Imprint my stunted mind
with your grace. I will receive you.

And the little slaughter starts anew.
The sweat the nausea the cold fingertips the agony of
                                                    the bones
and the sabbath of wondrous abstractions
in the horror of scarification.
The usual mournful peacock named Scheherazade
spreads her fan of piercings,
feathers and floras immediately petrified
in the vertigo of colours against nature, a lacerating
                                                    lynching
of sharp pointed stones. No way out.
The range of the unlimited is another jailhouse law
more perverse than any limit. Yet again
from beyond a glacial era the daily norm
resurfaces now & then with its poor homely face
while the merging of the kingdoms of nature
melts the veins in waves like the first childhood
                                                    menstruum
until the lymph is burnt. The carnal fever is consumed.
By now consciousness is but a moth beating around
                                        in the noxious darkness
searching for a thread of substance. Summer's dead.
Farewell farewell contact details & addresses popes
                            menageries & numbering systems,
Via della Scimmia, Navona, Avenue Americas.
Fare ye well measures, directions, five senses. Fare ye
                    well slavish duties & slavish rights & slavish
                                                    judgements.
Take shelter blindly on the other side, underworlds or
                                        limbos it won't matter,

rather than finding yourself in your sleazy domicile
where you squash yourself between the walls
                              smirched with painted canvases
that are recognized as rags & dusts of degraded
                              Shrouds.
The floor is a bloodied silt boiling up
to the rooms, decomposing ossuaries, in the last flash
of a warped brass plate where lemons
swell out into plastic bubbles. And from the mirror,
staring at you out of dusty eye-rings, something other
                              and yet
closely intimate, a dark scale on this side of every
                              incarnation,
negates even the skeleton and the whole vicissitude
of geneses epiphanies
sepulchres & easters. Don't try the crippled
ruinous route of the ladder, which for you is an ascent
                              of centuries
always with hell above & hell below.
The decayed sky is the ragged low tent
of the earthly plague house. And the Mozart flute
is an evil *saltarello*, its rivet reaching
all the way into your eyeball with its tawdry pantomime
of an obsessive arithmetics devoid of any other
                              meaning . . .
No further sky is uncovered. No thousand-petal lotus
                              unfolds.
You are all here, woman. And there's nothing else.
Attend to this. And stop calling out

for dead lovers, dead mothers.
Stripped bare, even poorer than you, they do not come
to this or any other dimension. Only your memory is left
as their ultimate dwelling.

    Memory memory, you house of punishment
where ugly big rooms & deserted landings echo
with the blare of loudspeakers whose stuck mechanism
won't stop replaying the bitter point
of unanswered Eli Elis. The howl of the boy
who crashes down blinded by the sacred sickness.
The young murderer writhing in the deranged dormitory.
The Christian litany cut short in the hospital
store room, around the dead old Jewess
who'd waved the cross away with her delirious little hands.
WITHOUT THE COMFORTS OF RELIGION. This house is
                                  full of blood
but blood itself, all bloods, are nothing but larval vapours
conforming to the mind that bears witness to them.
And when the time of the requiem comes for you, so will
                           it come for those howls.
The unconsecrated Sunday fades away
the plague moons are waning already
the hedge of thorns sends forth new shoots, your senses
                        peal out in five voices.
Hasten back, hasten back to meet your poor humdrum
                          tomorrows,
your deathbound workaday body.
It's supper time. O hunger for life, feed again
on the daily substance of slaughters.

Be born anew to forms & shared secrets & arbitrary choruses
to consciousness
to health
to the order of dates
to your own place.

No Revelation (Even when illegal, the show
always depends on the collective manufacturing of the
arbitrary).
No sin (The contraption designed for torture carries no
blame for the tortures, O poor sinners). And no special
grace.
(The only common grace is patience
until the amen of consummation).
Go in peace, woman. Absolved, absolved, although a
reoffender.
Good evening, good evening.
This Sunday too is gone.

III

The Evening at Colonus

A PARODY

O bristling star running with no alighting point
from a terrible starting point that does not exist.

MARINA TSVETAEVA

O she-cats,
beloved she-cats!

TORQUATO TASSO
(in Sant'Anna)

Antefactum

With its disquieting pronouncements, the cult of the Sun (god of light, of beauty, of prophecy and of the plague, also called—among his other numberless names—Apollo or Phoebus) moves Laius, King of Thebes, to eliminate his new-born son Oedipus; and, later, young Oedipus himself to flee from the adoptive family that had fortuitously saved him (an unknown and unaware child) from immolation at the hands of his father. But, as is well known, flight cannot save Oedipus from his fate, which has marked him as parricidal, incestuous and king of the city of seven gates. Until one day, recognizing the plague that ravages the city as a sign of his own guilt and of the solar curse, Oedipus blinds himself with a pin belonging to his suicide mother-wife, and sentences himself to begging and exile, dragging himself with no direction around the land, accompanied by his daughter Antigone.

The last predestined station, where he will find his end and his burial, is Colonus, a place sacred to the Furies, daughters of the Night (also called the Eumenides, i.e. the Benign).

It's from Him, my friends, that all my trouble comes.

Oedipus Rex

Near evening, in a mild mellow November, around the year 1960; inside a polyclinic in a South European city, in a corridor next to the neurological ward, situated on the ground floor. The whitewashed corridor measures roughly 11 yards by 3. On the left-hand side, a large double swing-door painted a glossy white leads to the nearby facilities and to the other wards. On the right-hand side (corresponding to the outer northern border of the hospital) a dark hallway gives access to a descending flight of stairs, the first steps of which are visible.

The place is lit by the bluish glare of a long neon tube, fixed above the door on the left-hand side. A different electric glow, of a dim reddish hue, filters in from the next ward through two small fanlights, armed with bars and set very high into the common wall. Against this wall, under the

fanlights, is a long white bench (the only furniture in the corri-
dor) on which are sat the THREE WARDERS, *ordinary stolid types*
in standard-issue tunics.

There are no openings to the outside. But through the walls, from
beyond the precinct, faint traffic noises can be heard; while from
the next ward, close by and relentless through the common wall,
comes the din of the CHORUS *of inmates. It is a babel of voices,*
deadened by tranquillizers and standard medication, each
engaged in its own monologue, all ringing out (among yawns,
coughing, etc.) in a sort of discordant, raving litany.

CHORUS

And the house, kaput! Good morning how's it going?
Good morning how's it going? Over four hundred and
fifty contestants—Fire!—Good morning how's it
going? You didn't stop at the Stop sign—I mustn't
think mustn't think—
Over four hundred and fifty contestants—The heart
has stopped. I mustn't think mustn't think mustn't
think mustn't think mustn't think—
Because the food was spoilt. One moment. May I take a
deep breath please? Thank you. One moment. That's
better. And the house, kaput! Good morning how's it
going?
We are all in the military!!! One moment TB—because
when the wafer bleeds it is a sign of importance.—What
do you want from me?! One moment one moment one
moment. One moment. One moment.
What notary deed? The heart has stopped—Good
morning how's it going?—With the maschinenpistole.

Lake Tana we're in Africa Siberia a stronghold in Africa—I want to ride on the Vespa for a whole stage like in the Tour—Fire!—May I breathe please? Thank you. Shall I cut a piece? Them nice childhood memories Bambi Disney. One moment one moment. For security reasons.—There's a holograph with a later date here.—With the maschinenpistole. Monday evening.

Do you know the American skeletons?

Ouch! Ouch! IN TLATELOLCO. What do *you* want from me? One moment one moment—May I take a breath, please? Thank you. That's better—

I mustn't think mustn't think.

Etc. While the CHORUS *continues as above, an electric bell rings, and the* FIRST WARDER *momentarily leaves the room.*

Presently the double door swings open and two porters enter with a stretcher, on which OEDIPUS *lies strapped. His forehead and eyes are wrapped in bandages soiled at the edges with tiny bloodstains; and his head is thrown back, in a tangle of thick curly hair of a woolly grey-white colour. He is breathing heavily, loose-lipped, deep in a sick, almost indecent, old man's sleep.*

Hurrying after the stretcher comes ANTIGONE, *a wild, trembling girl of about 14, but underdeveloped for her age. The* FIRST WARDER *follows, on his way back in.*

ANTIGONE (*whispering to the porters who are setting the stretcher on the floor*)
　. . . Please sir go easy don't throw 'im about sir
　cos 'e needs to sleep to get over the sickness innit—

it's
a good job 'e got to get to sleep cos this insomnia thing
is the worst trouble for 'im cos 'e can't get to
sleep like . . .

Exeunt the two porters.

FIRST WARDER *(to the other two who have sat down)*
His daughter.
The Doctor gave her permission
to stay overnight, considering his
critical condition . . .

Sits back down beside the others.

ANTIGONE
What's this? . . . you gonna leave 'im 'ere on the floor,
    in the corridor?!

FIRST WARDER
Well? where else?
Owing to the usual seasonal epidemics
there isn't a single free bed in the whole hospital.
We're having to rig up cots
and put mattresses on the floor
in the toilets and on the landings, even.
We've not a single spare cot or mattress left
owing to the overcrowding.

SECOND WARDER
That's normal, isn't it, at this time of the year.
When winter comes—as the old song goes—
the flies start dropping.

FIRST WARDER

And then this one, you know—he's obviously a
double special case. Obviously
we can't have him on the ward.
Out of the question. And whereabouts, anyway?
Here, in the dorm?!

SECOND WARDER

With the whole gang!!

FIRST WARDER

Out of the question.

THIRD WARDER

This case calls for special
isolation.

FIRST WARDER

That's right.

ANTIGONE

But there's too many voices in 'ere, like . . .

                              too many voices . . .
they're gonna wake 'im up . . .

FIRST WARDER

Nah—no chance of that, with the shot
the doctor gave him back in reception.

SECOND WARDER

Guaranteed not to wake up—
not if they carpet-bombed the whole place.

ANTIGONE

Yeah but medicinen't do nuffin for 'im sir you know
'e's like someone locked up in a room wiv the blinds
                              always up so you can't sleep cos 'e
        dreams it's always daylight even at night sir &
                                                  that's why

'e can't get to sleep innit . . .

FIRST WARDER

For the moment
seeing as we've an emergency situation at the hospital
the order is to leave him out here, pending
transfer.
It's a temporary provision.
We're sure to fix him up with a place
before the night is out.

ANTIGONE

Alright but please sir do me this favour at least—don't
                              leave 'im 'ere like that
wiv 'is feet facing the door
you know it's not good to lie like that when you're sick
                                                  it's like

bad luck innit.

SECOND WARDER

It's better to leave him where he his—comfortable.
Anyway, over here, the bad way out
is not through the door or even the main gate,
it's through that hole over there, down the side
                                        stairs.

ANTIGONE

Oh—where does that lead, then?

THIRD WARDER

Well, it goes down to the premises . . . down below . . .

SECOND WARDER

. . . where it's . . . cooler.

CHORUS (*continuing as above from the next ward*)

A whole stage on the Vespa, like at the Tour—What do *you* want?—One moment

one moment one moment—An electric-controlled switchboard. And now my friends let me tell you a little story or two—One moment—The heart has stopped— TB that goddamned tuba—I have destroyed a work of art, a painting—

Do you know the Table of Pythagoras?—Honour thy mother and father—A stronghold-church in Africa Lake Tana . . . —I don't want to think don't want to think —What do *you* want?—May I breathe please? Thank you . . .

Etc.

ANTIGONE (*to the warders*)

Trouble is, we live too far innit
but if we could take 'im back home
you know I could do it, take 'im back I mean, cos

maybe

'e'll be all right to walk when 'e wakes up you know we
walked miles & miles together we did—
sir, you know if you make it so that they let us go

back
to our house
we can make it worf your while sir you know my Pa's all
right back home I mean 'e's got two farms one with
olive trees
and a vineyard and a orange garden
cos my Pa's not some lowlife is 'e—sir, my Pa's got
a property that's 'is property 'e's the owner of 'is own
stuff you know
I mean for respectable like 'e's better 'n a teacher or
even a lord you know
'e's not like some people always depending, 'e can like—
dispose of 'is own stuff you know
and wiv 'is property as the property owner 'e don't have
to kiss up
to nobody.

The THREE WARDERS *remain inert on the bench; they've given up
on her and don't bother to reply.*

ANTIGONE
Sir!
I got a letter of recommendation 'ere—I mean this letter
is a letter of recommendation from the other doctor
the one that saw 'im at the other hospital a while ago you
know 'e
wrote it 'imself—the doctor I mean—'e remembered my
Pa 'e'd met 'im before
when they were on reserve
in the military like.

She pulls a soiled and crumpled sheet out of her sleeve.

FIRST WARDER (*takes the sheet and glances at it indifferently*)
Ah, yes—

you should have given it to the Assistant, not to us . . .

Hands the sheet to the SECOND WARDER.

SECOND WARDER (*glancing sullenly at the sheet between his fingers*)
Though

you might have looked after it a bit better, don't you
think—the way you've mangled it,
it mucks you up just to touch it . . .

ANTIGONE
That's the sweat sir
you know we walked miles & miles
you know after 'e—after my Pa messed up 'is eyes like
that wiv 'is own hands
'e can't see a thing as long as 'e's like that (cos you
know that effect 'e gets that 'e sees some things
for real
like they're really there it gives 'im trouble like, you
know 'e'll talk to them things but that's just the
feverish
cos really 'e
can't see no road
or no places
or no nuffin innit) so anyway
after that misfortune 'e needed to—like lean on some-
one—or how could 'e manage?and good job!
I was there

and of course I was sweating like—always carrying
                              that letter
in my sleeve
cos you know when we left home all in a rush in the
middle of the night 'e didn't give me no time
to take a bag or like a suitcase or anything he just said
        to me let's go Annie let's go and good job
I had this letter well safe in my bedside drawer so I
                snatched it up on the way out and
of course it got a little chewed up & sweaty like . . .
                        Sir, are you telling me it's
too filthy to be any good now?!

THIRD WARDER (*looking over the sheet, with a bleak laugh*)
    Well—actually, as documents go,
    it's good all right . . .

ANTIGONE
    What's in it, sir? please? what's it say?

The SECOND WARDER *submits the letter to the* THIRD WARDER
*who barely looks at it as he holds it passively in his hand like some-
one who has no use for it.*

ANTIGONE
    Eh? what's it say then? sir?

THIRD WARDER
    You mean . . . you can't read? . . .

ANTIGONE
    Yes I can a little . . . not very much tho . . . cos
    school things like . . . memory things I
    find 'em hard to remember like . . .

THIRD WARDER (*listless, struggling and expressionless, reads one syllable at a time, as if repeating a school lesson without understanding its meaning*)

... half rubbed out here ... Age ... 63 ... Small
        holder, good income ... A widower
with 4 children ... Judicial interdiction applied
                                   for
by his two sons ... both of age ...
Diagnosis ... paranoid delirium
syndrome ... Toxic psychosis of the ... hex-ogen?
end-ogen type? Alcoholic ... Suspected
user of narcotics ... addiction ... Severe uremic
complaints from alcoholism ... Severe
insomnia ... Little or no reaction tranquillizers
                      & sleeping pills ...
Status! Visual and auditory
hallucinations ... mis-recognizing people and
                  places & dis-oriented
as to time ... filthy ... clastomaniac ... Logorrheic ...
bombastic ... verbal stereotyping of a
pseudo-literary style ... peppered with classi-
cal quotes ... Verbal flow char-ac-ter-ized by
long mon-odies of a pseudo-litur-gic or epic
intonation ... Struc-tured del-irium contents
... Aggressive fits ... myth-omania ...
                Mannerisms ... Flights
of fancy ...
Precedents! farming family ... Father fallen
First World War ... Subsequent mother's suicide at
P. H. ... As a child the subject showed religious

inclinations . . . Admitted to seminary . . .
Interrupted studies . . . ran away . . . Emigrated
Colonies agricultural . . . worker . . . South America
                                . . . Petty officer . . . fought
Second World War in Africa . . . where seem-ing-ly
                                        gained sinister
distinction for
excesses of cruelty and violence against prisoners and
natives . . . Subsequently taken prisoner transferred
                                        various
camps . . . occasion attempted escape wounded by
a lookout . . . consequent bone deformation . . .
                tarsus . . . metatarsus . . . Returned
homeland. 1945–46 shaken by much
misfortune in the family . . . first signs disturbed
behaviour peaking last crisis following
recent bereavement . . . a widower . . . formerly
                                        admitted
for observation . . .

ANTIGONE

That's all because of the misfortune sir!!
cos everyone's always known 'im 'e never
did no cruelty!!! 'e never took anybody's
stuff!! you know 'e's got a vineyard &
a orange garden & the house 'n' all—'e's
learnt it all for 'imself working in Lamerica innit 'e's
learnt 'is property with sacrifice you know
if it wasn't for the misfortune sir cos that was
                        because of the heartbreak

of the misfortune cos my mother Sandoro Agnese
flew off to heaven she deceased on a
                              Sunday night and 'e
never expected this blow like—thirty years she lived
                              wiv 'im
like two bodies & one soul but in front of 'er poor
          body 'e couldn't say a thing you know
'e looked like a puppet the poor thing & then
'e went down to the grotto and skulled two or three
                              flasks of wine at least
and then 'e went to sleep for one day & one night &
                              more
that's why 'e lost all 'is memory of things innit &
                              then one night
'e ups & wakes me up & says let's go let's go and me
                              and 'im just like that
we walked miles & miles
& miles
cos my Pa's a great walker, sir! never mind that
                              problem wiv 'is feet
also, that problem's not a birth thing sir you know
that was cos of 'is hero's decoration for the
                    fatherland innit, cos 'e was recalled
                              to the army you know
cos that was wartime I weren't even born—good
                    job that! or I'd have died
of heartache to see 'im go away
fit as a fiddle & come back all lamed but 'e's still a
                    great walker you know

we walked miles 'n' miles & my Pa explained to me
  that there's no other cure for the nancient curse you
      know that 'e was born
under the curse of Phoebus lord of earth 'n' sky
and so 'e's got to go gypsying around begging
always hunting down that wild lamb
cos that's like a nancient debt innit: eever 'e pays
    the sacrifice of the debt
or 'e's always in trouble! what do I know?! 'e knows
    everything like
cos 'e's read allthebooks that alltheothers don't
      understand much like
cos 'e's not like alltheothers stuck in the village
     filling their faces 'e's
been everywhere, to Lamerica 'n' everywhere 'e's a
    great traveller you know
'e was a commander as well with the rank of
  sergeant you know 'e's still got 'is
      stripes back home sir and then
'e's picked up the speaking from everywhere but
   now because of that thought that got into 'is 'ead
'e's speaking a different language that's like
music & he sounds like a foreigner
or a singer like
so we were walking miles & miles
then
that morning—you know, eleven twelve o'clock
'e disappeared behind that wall 'n' I thought 'e
  was like answering the call of nature

but then I saw 'im come out wiv 'is face all
    bloodied up & a broken bottle in 'is hand
you know 'e says it was two nails but I thought it
    was a broken bottle cos at that moment I was
seeing double so scared I was 'n' screaming worse
    'n 'im I was screaming: 'Pa,

                what have you done?!'
but then when I saw 'e'd' gone 'n' passed out on
        me I washed 'im down with water
and 'e pulled 'imself together & then I said to 'im
    it's nuffin, look I'm 'ere, here, lean on me it's
           nuffin
cos you know 'e really trusts me cos you know
even if our home is too far from 'ere I
I think I could manage to take 'im back home
that if it 'adn't been for alltheothers who got
        scared of 'im
if it 'adn't been that they took 'im by force
still you know even in that state of blindness
    they couldn't catch 'im you know, seven or
        eight against 'im all alone
but we could've been home now and not in 'ere you
        know that the worst thought
for 'im was always that! to end up in the nervous
        delirium hospital
that he was scared of that worse than being sent
        down—good job
I was allowed to stay over wiv 'im now cos all right
I can't help 'im that much but at least

'e's not all alone cos that's the worst heartache
                    when you're disabled innit,
to be all alone cos when you're disabled the most
                    important thing is
to have some family close by innit
for assistance like.

The THREE WARDERS, *who no longer bother listening to her,*
remain voiceless and expressionless in their indolent poses
while on the other side of the dividing wall the CHORUS *con-*
tinues its relentless confabulations as above. Haggard and
bewildered, ANTIGONE *draws near the bench, and with the*
sudden quickness of a cat, snatches back the famous 'letter of
recommendation' left there by the warders and jealously stows
it back safe in her sleeve. Then she resolves to sit on the far
corner of the bench, perched on the very edge, but immediately
thinks better of it, jumps back up, takes off her little overcoat
and, spreading it on the floor next to the stretcher, sits down
and settles herself there.

ANTIGONE (*reasoning with herself*)
    It's not cold in 'ere anyway with the heating on—
            it's not even cold outside—good job it's
    nice weather for winter & then I mustn't get
            scared in 'ere that's the main thing
    not to get scared like cos it takes
    patience innit.

In a fussy little manner, she shifts to a more comfortable posi-
tion on her overcoat.

CHORUS (*as above*)

Disjointed bones ... You have to write all the figures
in Roman numerals—Over four hundred contestants
and zeropointfifty ... —One moment one moment one
moment one moment ... —In Tlatelolco in Tlat-el-ol-
co ... —I can smell poison gas—Show your card—
Fire!!!—We must all turn into killing machines—
killing machines—
We're in Cloud Cuckoo Land here—One moment
one moment—
May I breathe please? May I
take a deep breath please? Thank you—Show me
this
photograph!! three dimensions—In
Tlatelolco ... —With the maschinenpistole—
There are machines following me ... —A four-
dimensional cinema ... —Shall I cut
a piece?

Etc.

OEDIPUS (*stirring, with a lament of almost indecent abjection*)
Owwwww ... Oww, ow ...

Precisely at the moment of OEDIPUS' *awakening, the* CHORUS'
*previous 'real' vociferations turn into an enormous unison
echoing his lament: resounding deafeningly, but 'blurred' and
disturbed by unnatural interferences—as if produced by a
gramophone record played at maximum volume but warped
with wear and sticking at times.*

CHORUS (*in a mechanical, echoing unison*)
Owwwwwww ... Ow, ow ...

OEDIPUS (*writhing and struggling with the restraining straps*
    holding him down on the stretcher)
    Owwwww owwww ah
    damn you sun you cursed drunken sun you fanatical
                                                    sun
    you boozed-up unkempt drugged-up demented sun
                                                writhing
    in the sky. Go,
    base old sun, go, you murderous hustler tied up and
                            shoving around in the
    sky,
    go away stop it
    stop, stop it . . .

ANTIGONE
    Pa!
    Don't thrash around like that Pa, you'll open up
                    your wounds again, look, your bandage
    is soaking in blood, Pa! Rest your head
    on the pillow—look I promise you, the sun's
                    gone now, believe in my eyes believe in
                            my voice Pa, it's been dark
    for more 'n an hour now.

OEDIPUS
    No! HE is always tied up there always stuck in
                            the middle of the sky.
    It's always midday, always the time fixed
    for his ugly ghosts with their horses' hooves
    to bar up the way out of all precincts. HE keeps
                                            me

inside his barbed wires . . . accused of contumacy.
I have to chase contumacy out of the den . . .

(*Turning round, facing the* THREE WARDERS)

   . . . Who are you, standing there, barking
with three heads and one body?

THREE WARDERS (*jumping up, stiff and tight together, as if
   bolted to one another, spelling words out in one voice, with
   the alien accent of automatons*)
I am
the three-headed hound guarding the river that
                        flows underground.
No way through here, without a document of
                           baptism
and of burial.

OEDIPUS (*still addressing the three*)
You wouldn't happen to have seen
a little wolf cub, lame and marked with two
                   crosses on its forehead?

THREE WARDERS (*all together as above*)
Yes, I have seen him running and hiding
there
in the
rubble.

OEDIPUS
Get him! Go for him! That's
the murderer! Get him!

THREE WARDERS (*as above*)
    You cannot catch him. He is camouflaged. You
                cannot make him out in this sun
    that turns everything white.

OEDIPUS
    Hunt him down! Get him!

ANTIGONE
    Pa! Pa, listen to me! rest your head on the pillow
                Pa stop tiring yourself out
    wi' this hunt business—you know
    it's not a good time anyway now it's dark & all
                        the animals've turned inside & gone to
                                                    sleep.
    Trust me, I'm telling you the truth, it's been dark
                        for more 'n an hour now.

OEDIPUS (*falling into a reverie*)
    There's a bounty on the runaway murderer . . . I
    want to buy myself a tent in the shade
                                    with it . . .
    Here under the sun, the channels of pestilence
                                    multiply . . .
    But it's all the fault of that marked little cockerel
                                    hiding away!
    He is the plague staining
    all this rubble with blood. We must search for him
    under the rubble. He's alive, breathing.

ANTIGONE
    There's no rubble 'ere Pa—you know we're in a

nice place now on a nice night, we
are in a nice garden on a nice night, believe my
    eyes dear father all this stuff you're saying
is not true—that's all a—a ecstasy you've got
                    because of the wounds
of your poor crippled eyes
so it's like you're like half asleep
Pa.

OEDIPUS

What's down there?
What's that hole?

ANTIGONE

Oh, that . . . ?
That's a—
a nice fountain wi' statues
wiv a lectric lighting hiding inside it
what makes the water look like all nice colours!

OEDIPUS

Ah here they come again
the buildings, the rail tracks, the people . . .

ANTIGONE

Yeah but that's just cos you're like half asleep
Pa.

Meanwhile the THREE WARDERS *have sat on the bench
again, returning to their normal shapes and to the same
indolent postures as before.*

CHORUS

Over four hundred and fifty contestants . . . I
mustn't think mustn't think mustn't think —Good
morning how's it going?—Good morning how's it
going?—Fire!—You have to write all the figures
down in Roman numerals—I've bought a red
ribbon— I've bought—When the wafer bleeds it
is a sign of importance—a red ribbon—Show
your card—Over four hundred and fifty thousand
contestants—I've bought a red ribbon—One
moment—May I breathe please?—One moment
one moment—You didn't stop at the Stop sign—
IN TLATELOLCO—With the maschinenpistole—
May I take a deep breath please? Thank you.

OEDIPUS

These huge crossings of so many equators
alternate inside me with a different nausea: the
                    flat measurements of an insect
walking along a crack.
I don't want this skewed, peeling whitewashed
                    wall in front of me any more
all streaked with stains and buzzing
with words . . . What language do they speak?
Where am I?! . . .
Where have you taken me?!

ANTIGONE

That's not a wall, Pa
that is a
a beautiful gateway of roses

you know you mustn't believe your impressions,

> Pa

that's just the feverish mixing
everything up like things & noises you know
it's just the feverish
mixing you up
innit Pa.

Enter a DOCTOR, *in haste, accompanied by an assistant.*

THREE WARDERS (*standing up lazily*)
Evening, doc.

DOCTOR (*raising his hand briskly in reply*)
Any news?

THREE WARDERS
Nothing.

CHORUS
Over four hundred and fifty contestants—For security
reasons.—I've bought a red ribbon—One moment one
moment—Thank you—I've bought a red ribbon—I
want to go a whole stage on the Vespa—Where are you
parked?—I've bought a red ribbon—Good morning
how's it going?—One moment one moment. IN
TLATELOLCO—OW! OWW!—Over four contestants—
IN TLATELOLCO
THE FIRE TURNS BLACK

The DOCTOR, *barely glancing at* OEDIPUS, *shrugs helplessly and
exchanges a few whispered words with the* ASSISTANT. *Then, as
the* ASSISTANT *exits, he jots down notes in a prescription book.*

ANTIGONE (*between shy and diffident, sidles up to the* DOCTOR *and pulls him by the sleeve*)
Doc . . .

The DOCTOR *turns absent-mindedly to look at her.*

ANTIGONE
Like please doc if we could
loosen up the straps on 'im a little bit . . . on 'is
arms at least? cos you know it's
more trouble for 'im to be so tied up like.

DOCTOR (*shaking his head curtly*)
It is a basic
and indispensable precaution, in the patient's
own interest.

Continues taking notes.

ANTIGONE *hesitates for an instant about giving him the* '*letter of recommendation*' *but out of diffidence refrains. Then she returns hurriedly to* OEDIPUS' *side; he has resumed his lamentations, swinging his head in a sort of stupor.*

OEDIPUS (*moaning*)
Owwwwwwww . . . Owwwww . . .

CHORUS (*suddenly erupting into the same lament, in* OEDIPUS' *own voice, multiplied in unison at an enormously high register, as if through a loudspeaker*).
Ow, ow . . . Owwwwww . . .

OEDIPUS (*addressing the* DOCTOR)
Who are you?
I think I recognize you

from the crown of gold
you wear . . .

DOCTOR (*suddenly stiffening like a wooden puppet and speaking
in a mechanical syncopated voice*)
I am
the king of this country. I too now recognize you
from your gouged and bloodied eye sockets
O self-punisher, O unfortunate son of Laius.
Many have told me your story, with the news
of your imminent arrival.

OEDIPUS

What kingdom is this you rule? . . .

KING

This is the land consecrated to the holy daughters
of darkness,
they of the many names.
They live down below, they have their church in
this place.
In our parts they are known by the name
of Benign Ones
or Erinyes,
and elsewhere
some call them Furies, some Insult, some Fear.

OEDIPUS

O Merciful Ones
so I have arrived
at the unknown station that was promised:
perhaps to my rest? In the oracle by HIM, that
same one

where ever since the beginning, clear in the reading
—now I recognize it!—my relentless toiling
was ordained,
there is a part that was scratched off, under the
                                        sign
of your hallowed name.
What that part would portend for me, I
can never recall,
and that doubtful point is by now
the one nesting place of my hope.
O creatures of the night,
you who have seen every writing deciphered
ever since ever in your sweet mantle of eyes
you eternal witnesses, noiseless fleeing, vibratile
                                        hair, little velvet foot,
refuge of murderers, keepers of the hidden arks,
                                        you
divine nyctalopes, give shelter in your realm
to this old man.

*The sound of a little bell is heard from somewhere in the hospital.
The* DOCTOR, *resuming his ordinary form and functions, leaves
the corridor, followed by the* THREE WARDERS.

CHORUS

Disjointed bones . . . —Good morning how's it
going?—A guy shadowing me, ringing bells . . . —
Show your card—We're in Cloud Cuckoo Land here—
We're all in the military—One moment one
moment—I want to go one whole stage like in the
Tour . . . —I've bought a lucky red ribbon . . . —Show
your card—

Etc.

OEDIPUS *weeps silently.*

ANTIGONE (*crouched by his side again, on her little overcoat*)
    Pa
    you know how I wish I could take your pain on me
    cos it's breaking my heart to see you so ill
    cos I'd give anything to make it come now, that day
    when I can see you well again like you used to be
        & look into your eyes bright as two pretty stars
    like they used to be—cos you know
    Pa, I'm still hoping that all that stuff about your
                sight not comin' back—well—maybe
    the doctors got it all wrong—you know they make
                    mistakes sometimes Pa
    like that time with me you remember
    when the doctor said that feverish I had 'e said it
        was some contagious—like—'pidemic innit
    but it was just cos I'd eaten too much seafood innit
                             Pa
    that's an example frexample
    innit Pa?

OEDIPUS *falls asleep again.* ANTIGONE *leaves the room for a moment and returns with a bottle of water and a glass which she places on the floor next to the invalid. Then, having sat down again, she rummages in the pocket of the overcoat spread under her, pulls out a small paper bag and (facing the wall lest she disturb the sick man) starts eating her bread and cheese, not forgetting the crumbs that fall from it. After which she settles back into her original position. At this moment, no one else is in the corridor.*

CHORUS *(continuing as above)*
We are all in the military—With the maschinen-
                                        pistole—This is
Cloud Cuckoo
Land—I've bought a red ribbon
You have to write all the figures down in Roman
                                        numerals—One moment
one moment

Etc.

The double door swings open again: enter two porters, carrying a litter with a body stretched out on it and covered by a sheet. Opposite, in the narrow stairwell, a neon light is switched on. The porters start down the stairs with the litter. After a moment, the stairwell plunges back into darkness.

From now on, the normal bustle of hospital service rooms will continue in the corridor. At intervals, the THREE WARDERS *will exit and re-enter, now alternating, now finding themselves again sitting together, now standing—in turn—on the bench to keep watch over the dormitory from the fanlights, etc. Now and again nurses, cleaners, etc., will pass through.*

But OEDIPUS *will remain mostly inured to these 'actual' events. Only sporadically will he regain a fragmentary perception of them, and these fragments of 'ordinary reality' will frighten him more than anything else.*

Not far from the corridor, a door is heard to slam; then electric bells ringing from some ward, etc.

CHORUS (*as above*)

> Some guy shadowing me, ringing bells . . . —We're in Cloud Cuckoo Land here.— There are lots of machines following me—Good morning how's it going?—Show your card—I've bought a lucky red ribbon, and tried to eat it, but could only chew it.

Whistles, coughing, etc.

OEDIPUS (*starting awake*)

> Where am I?!

ANTIGONE

> Pa, are you thirsty? Do you want a drink? Look, I
>   got water for you—

Carefully lifts his head from the pillow, offering sips of water to his lips. But OEDIPUS *starts with a convulsive movement, spilling part of the water on the sheet.*

OEDIPUS

> Who's this screaming? Why is everyone rushing
>   over?! What does all this crowd want
> from me?

ANTIGONE

> No Pa, don't thrash around like that, you're
>   gonna ruin yourself—I told you before Pa,
> remember? that you must believe me, that
>   there's
> nothing wrong 'ere, you mustn't get all worked
> up with bad ideas Pa, cos that's just the
>   feverish

mixing everything up Pa, that's
the feverish
mixing you up innit

CHORUS (*continuing as above*)

One moment one moment one moment—You
didn't stop at the Stop sign!—One moment—Show
me this 3D photograph!—Let's make a four-dimen-
sion character and you get the hell out of the Roman
Forum!!—May I breathe please? Thank you.

Etc.

OEDIPUS (*calling out in a loud voice*)

Antigone!
Antigone!!

ANTIGONE

I'm right here Pa listen, this is my voice
this is my hand stroking your hair Pa—you
    know there's no one else 'ere, just me
your daughter Annie
there's nuffin to scare you here Pa it's all in your
                                  mind you know—it's nuffin,
nuffin at all.

CHORUS (*as above*)

I want to go one whole stage with the Vespa—With
the maschinenpistole—Like at the Tour!—For secu-
rity reasons—One moment one moment—Because
the food was spoilt —One moment one moment one
moment—Over four hundred and fifty thousand

contestants—OW! OW! STAND BY
                                    ME
                    DIVINE WATER BLAZING!

OEDIPUS
    Where
    are we? . . .

ANTIGONE (*in a frightened, lilting voice*)
    We are
    we're under a pretty little arbour of trees Pa
    in a lovely foreigner square I don't know what it's
                                    called cos it's
    foreigner right?
    but this square is all made up of gorgeous
                        gardens & in the evening like now
    it's like a riot of lights with roundabouts & music
                        & fortune-tellers & floats & all!
    And there's a little puppet show on as well, like
                        down in Pescherìa, remember?
    And a rollercoaster even, wiv lectric cars of all
                                    different colours
    and a raffle too, with price-winning & a crowd of
                                    people
    buying everything & coming & going & talking
                                    to their families
    and meeting up & joking around with their
                        mates 'n' 'aving a good time
    and milling around . . .

CHORUS (*as above*)

There's a holograph here with a later date—Do you know the Table of Pythagoras?—I don't want to think don't want to think—It's an electric-controlled switchboard. May I breathe please? May I take a deep breath? Oh thank you—One moment one moment—With a later date—You have to write all the figures down in Roman numerals—Where are you parked?—This should be printed in the newspaper—One moment—

GO DOWN OLE MAN—WELL, WELL,
WELL

YOU GO DOWN MASTER OF HEAVEN
& DON'T YOU RISE AGAIN!

OEDIPUS (*dreamily, his head lolling*)

They're all ghosts. If they were alive
they'd stop and stare, frightened
by this exotic pair, so strange to see:
an old beggar, a mass of base miseries
with two blood clots for eyes,
accompanied by a little gypsy, semi-feral and
dark-skinned like him,
a poor little slip of a girl, stunted on account of
her bad birth,
bearing on her face the sweet and repelling signs
of creatures
whose mind is slightly retarded . . .

ANTIGONE

. . . that's right, it's like

no one's taking any notice of us two innit! Every
one rushing past without stopping,
peeping from the door a moment then disappearing
just like the room was all empty . . .

OEDIPUS (*as above*)
The brain is a sly and idiotic machine nature made
for us, specially
designing it
to exclude us from the real show, and amuse
herself at our misunderstandings.
Only when the machine breaks down, in fevers,
in our death throes, do we begin
to make out a thread
of the forbidden scenario.
In my spasmodic and corrupted blindness I now
can see
things that are kept from innocent health,
from intact eyes . . .

CHORUS (*as above*)
THIS SHOULD BE PRINTED IN THE NEWS-
PAPER—A guy shadowing me . . . — Do you know
the American skeletons?—Show your card—My
hands, a worker's hands, should be printed in the
newspaper—Show your card—Shall I cut a
piece?—THIS IS
A GLORIOUS PAGE
IN OUR HISTORY. THE PEOPLE FROM
AIMANTLA ARE OUR
ENEMIES

HELP OUR IRON-CLAD LORDS.
Do you know the Table of Pythagoras?—ES
PANTAS AUDA!—Ninety-six centuries . . . —The
battleships . . . —WE SHALL ELIMINATE THEM
LIQUIDATE THEM IT'S EASY—Disjointed bones
. . . —ES PANTAS AUDA!!—I've bought a lucky
red ribbon . . .

Whistles, swearing, etc.

At intervals, these usual vociferations from the CHORUS
*seem to change their provenance and distance but in a
random and incongruous way. For example, the more
banal and gossip-like sentences may ring out like war cries
(or jubilant or insurgent cries) from huge and faraway
populations, resounding through wastelands of derelict
buildings or enormous cliffs. Conversely, 'historical' or
solemn or archaic or incomprehensible sentences may reach
us in a confidential whisper, or echo beside* OEDIPUS *as
if blaring out from a loudspeaker placed on his pillow.
The intonation too is entirely arbitrary and illogical. Cata-
strophic announcements (such as 'The heart has stopped!'
or 'And the house, kaput!' etc.) sound like merry surprises
. . . and so on, allowing for all possible combinations.*

OEDIPUS (*swinging his head around with a faint smile*)
So many people!
The theatre is full!
TODAY TOMORROW AND YESTERDAY . . .
I act because they pay me . . .

CHORUS

> You didn't stop at the Stop sign!—You are the guy
> who shadowed me, ringing bells . . . You didn't stop
> at the Stop sign!!—This
> is Cloud Cuckoo Land . . .

Etc.

OEDIPUS *(heaves a deep sigh—and swinging his head rhyth-*
mically, begins to SING in a theatrically inspired man-
ner, and in the monotone of a dirge such as can sometimes
be heard at village 'wakes')

> . . . TODAY TOMORROW and YESTERDAY are
> > three horses chasing one another
> round a circus track.
> The entire story is constantly enacted in the
> > vertiginous halo
> fixed and ever-changing order always fleeing
> > backwards.
> And here and there and nowhere now in the
> > eternal and in the never
> long-buried Thebeses and Jerusalems loom
> > newborn
> over the split second when Polis and City hit
> > rock bottom falling through light millennia
> and fuse into one phantom that varies
> like double Algol, demon of the sky.
> And the Christian calvary precedes the towers of
> > giants the sodoms and olympus mounts and
> > > elysiums
> yet follows them on the same merry-go-round.

There's no beginning or closure or order of

                                    sentences

as used in the writings

of syntactic logic.

AND DEATH AND BIRTH AND DEATH AND

      BIRTH AND DEATH AND BIRTH

this motto ever repeated in the same characters

                          with no commas or full stops

is printed round the circumference of a wheel.

But the mind, gripped in the vice of its

      fragmentary linear measure,

fabricates its own geographies and histories

like a locked-up madman who pacing the length

                        and breadth of his ward

thinks he is journeying to discover unexplored

                                 regions.

CHORUS (*continuing as above*)

    This should be printed in the newspaper—There

    are machines following me . . .

Etc.

Whistling, etc., as above.

OEDIPUS (*continuing his song as above*)

    . . . I alone, dragged by a furious impossible grief

    round the track of multiple dimensions

    on the whirling wheel of generations

    can see the cities all rising and falling on the

                          same spot,

    and architectures transmuting as if reeling at a

                                    drunken man's nauseas,
and bloods and pollens mixed together, and
    crowds coupling and squabbling
                                        and dancing
over the ravening burial where their bones
                                            crumble
and immediately reassemble as skeletons, and
                            are clad in flesh and hair
even at the same instant as they are twisted into
                                            corpses
and turned to dust again. I can see oarsmen's
                                            boats
sliding along the cold green current
of the combust grassland plain—and aquatic
                        fins beating in myriads
in the burning lavas of emerged volcanoes—and
    forests drenched in lymphs and seeds and saps
riding wild-haired
over the sierra of glass skyscrapers—and the
                            comets of the Magi
hurtling along the route of lunar ships
blurred in the dust of galaxies
and Hiroshimas—all in perpetuum
in a din of languages and workshops and steps
that has the horror of negative numbers,
    a tornado on this side of silence.
But the crux of the relentless suffering
that through my tendons' uneradicate ropes
                        nails me to the wheel's hub

is always there, one, always
the same: the city
of the plague.
Watched over by the sepulchral fairy
who lures with her trick, her risible enigma,
there it is—amid the crosses—
the gateway to the Orient
the womb
the promised palace!
Shuttle of eternal monotony
weaving ever anew the arabesque cloth of the
                                same anguish:
the end of fatherly kingdoms already inscribed
                        on the tiny unborn hands;
and the fatherly wars sending sons to the
                        slaughter to defraud fate;
and the angels tying the threads of oblique
                        oracles and winking alibis
around the unrecognizable consummation
at the three-way crossroads—because of the
                                returning necessity
that ties evil, grown unscathed and bloodthirsty
from the severed root of nature,
to the bridal feast contaminated by the double
                                infamy
and to the incurable farewell from the dead.
O Maia O Mary!
Now I no longer know if this identical scene of
                                my sickness

is a memory of something I've seen
or an omen of something I've yet to see.
I don't know if the plague is a consequence of the
            infamy, or its cause, or its pretext, or one of
                                    its dreams.
I don't know if Laius is guilty of Oedipus, or
            Oedipus of the father, or if the fault is
                                    Jocasta's,
nor if this old age weeping here and now is Laius,
            or Oedipus, or the mother, or them all,
                                    or all the others.
Perhaps, I am the body of each ancestor and each
                                    progeny
the blind and fixed abode of all the rotations of
                                    time
and the festering swarm of all contaminations.
True, this vicious noontide theatre
that has me spinning in its relentless windmill
might be but a conjuring trick of senile dementia
and nothing might be in front of me but a sense-
                                    less scrawl
daubed by an inmate on the hospital wall.
But the suffering is certain.
It is my very presence. It is mine.
I am not somebody looking upon the suffering
of this guy Oedipus. I *am*
this suffering . . .

CHORUS
Owwwww! Oooooooww!

OEDIPUS (*continuing as above*)
   . . . But the certainty of suffering cannot be
                                   explained
   to the tragic ear, where all sound
   barriers come crumbling down.
   In the desert lowlands, unattainable, nearer than
                          the pulse at my wrist
   and further away than the nebulae
   my howls race and collide through the vestibules
                            and labyrinths
   of soundless canyons
   and resound inaudible inside a sphere
   with no bones or bark.
   A hundred thousand rainbows paint the
                           vibrating range
   of all longitudes
   and all the words of my song, storied
   with circuses and horses and islands and tombs
                     and arthurs and mothers,
   are insubstantial little figures of a poor
                        provisional jargon
   that is not mirrored in the fantastic scriptures
   of Thrones and Dominions.
   Suffering and *beatitude*—*others* and *myself*
   all of these names are but fictitious differences
   that I can switch and swap around at will.
   I can call waking *sleep*; or myself *Legion*, ·
   and the others *Swellfoot*. I can say *tomorrow was*
   and dub this dried-up wall *the Palace of Thebes*.

I can dismember names and reassemble them all
        at random, creating out of them
                                monsters far stranger
than centaurs and chimerae.
I can abolish all known languages and invent
unheard-of others. Despoil many a
                                necropolis and barbarian
of their names.
I can ordain whole hierarchies of names,
venerate some as sacred, disdain others as filthy,
and subvert that order afterwards. Mix the words
                                of all vocabularies
into one chorus voicing curse or imploration,
or meditate on one name, reducing all others to
                                silence.
I can estrange myself from all verbal significance.
Vociferate in a language of mysteries like the
                        possessed or like the sibyls do.
Or ejaculate meaningless syllables. Or speak
                        forth nothing but numbers.
I can, rejecting articulated words for ever,
howl like the dumb, bark like a dog or whistle
                                like the wind . . .
. . . But all these revolutions belong to a status
of which there is no news
in the ranks of the unattainable court
—remote unattainable right next to me
                                unattainable.
The place of grace is the absence of all news

and every presence is an inferior place.
Memory,
like clairvoyance, is a sin.
Evil is a solitary question
mark in the void, an off-key voice in the silence
                                        of replies,
only survival of deaths and births and deaths.
It's me, that point of guilt.
No one denies death and goes unpunished. The
        grace of eternal death
only belongs to the unborn.
And the sentence served for being born
is to no longer be able to die.

CHORUS

Owwww . . . Oowwwww . . .
Show your card—My respects—Good morning
                                how's it going?
Is this transfusion really necessary?
The mirrors are covered by a sheet.—This is a
                    military zone—This is state property.

ANTIGONE

Pa
my dearest Pa what fault are you accusing
                                        yourself of
you know there is no father in the world as good
                                        as you
cos you always let me off innit
when I didn't want my hair combed & when I
                                forgot things

and when I robbed the pearls off of the Madam
and when I gave the cats our fresh sardines
and you always used to hit my brothers when
                                                                they hit me
what evil 'ave you ever done my poor old Pa
you've always worked so hard for all the family
and if it wasn't for this sickness
we'd all be sitting at home having our dinner
with my brothers & sister & everyone innit
Pa, the only evil you've ever done is
what you've gone & done to your poor eyes
but that too was because of the sickness innit
and you know sickness is not your fault but like a
                                                                misfortune, right?
that can happen to any good old body
not just you, innit Pa.

CHORUS

Oww . . . Owwww . . .
But is this transfusion really needed?
There's no smoking here—This is state property.
The mirrors are covered
with a sheet.

OEDIPUS

Farewell FAREWELL
is the only legible word on this defaced wall
that's my last home—a jailhouse eternity
with no more home fires nor any room for
                                                                meetings or returns.
Would that I were at least the heart of hearts

the gift of the long-awaited perishable solace
the deception of beauty one thanks like a charity.
Would that I were the standard-bearing kid
        rushing foolhardy and radiant into
                senseless battles
followed by legions of lovestruck madmen.
Would that I were the musics of a barrel organ, a
wandering bard of childhood fairs
or the festive lauds of a poor ultimate altar!
But oh to be the nerve of laceration
the blinded forehead keening for youths and
        mothers and rooms
Oedipus the cursed . . .

CHORUS

The transfusion's compulsory here—This is a
military zone—Ha ha I'm ticklish—The
           transfusion tax
is four hundred and fifty a litre—Zeroes
    don't count—Over four and a half
hundred contestants, that's five teaching posts—
    You didn't stop at the
Stop sign—this is
a military zone.—Show your card.—Ha ha I'm
ticklish—The transfusion comes at a fixed price
           it is a
monopoly commodity . . .

Whistling, laughing, sighing, etc.

Yeah but look, Pa—this worry about the dead is
                        just because of your memories innit
you mustn't cry about that! Cos actually you
        know the poor deceased are happy
about the memory—cos that's why you do the
                        keening innit—it's like memory, like
some signal that's lit up to let 'em know that even
                        if they're deceased
they're still part of the family just like they used
                        to be
all together in the family wiv us like it used to be,
                        so they can
remember us as well innit—so that's why the
        keening's good for them, it makes
them feel safer and happy
like
cos you know Pa, in this world death comes at
                        different timetables
that's natural innit—like at home at night you go
                        to sleep earlier, I go later and
sometimes people even squabble over that but
                        they don't cry cos I mean,
a half hour more or less is the same difference
                        innit
round eleven o'clock or midnight everyone's
                        asleep anyway . . .
and you know Pa
sometimes I think I see our life like it's a day—
                        one day I mean—

and first thing you start out from home like a
little beast on all 4s
cos the little critter can't walk by 'imself but
needs 'is mother to hold 'im up
but then round midday & the afternoon 2 legs
will do cos the young man is strong enough
on 'is own
but towards evening 'e can't hold 'imself up on 2
legs any more
cos old age is crippling 'im with arthuritis like
and so if 'e's stuck 'e makes do wiv 'a cane but
more better still
if 'e's got a kid I mean a son or evenly a daughter to
lean on
'e goes home in peace at dinnertime and then at night
everyone goes to sleep in peace together and the
day is done
and bedtime comes for everyone innit not just
people
but animals too & veg & wood & beef meat &
birds
I mean everyone who gets born must die cos like
a goat lives on grass
so death must live on people innit—mustn't grumble,
me
even if I am born to die
I'm glad I was born cos if I wasn't
I'd be the odd one out without no family but I'm
glad especially with you Pa now that you're old
I think if I wasn't born who'd look after you eh,

you know that's a disaster
when you're old if there's no company—you know an
old man
can't just be gypsying around all alone especially if
'e's mentally ill like
you know I think about it sometimes
and say to myself good job! that at least I'm near!!
cos look, Pa,
if it's for me you can be sure
I'm staying right here by your side I'm
not leaving you ever.

CHORUS

It's this guy who was shadowing me . . . —Who goes
there?—This is a military zone—You need a password
with the radio signal here—This is Cloud Cuckoo Land
. . . —Zimzimzim tralala taraboom da—
YITGADAL VEYITKADASH SHEMEH RABA
This is the sung Mass it's a Texas dance number . . .

OEDIPUS

Owww . . . Owwww . . .
. . . Here it goes again,
this loathsome lament! Who is it? Is it many voices
or one? . . .
. . . WHERE am I?!
Who's next door, screaming, strapped down on a
cot?!
Off with those ropes! Untie him! Saw through
his shackles! Here come the whistles,
the guards are here

with the handcuffs ... Get 'em! Shoot the guards!
... WHERE am I? where have you taken me!?
Antigone! Antigone!!

From outside, one of the THREE WARDERS *peeps between the door wings. Sound of steps. Ringing of bells.*

ANTIGONE

PA! I'm right here Pa!! Can you hear me, this is
my voice
this is my hand stroking your hair Pa—there's no
one in here just me
your daughter Annie
you know we're in a room with a window & a little
balcony over the road
and those voices—you mustn't believe them Pa,
it's all in your mind cos actually
that's noises in the street & people coming &
going & bicycles
with their bells ringing
and traffic warderers whistling & car horns you
know
—it's nuffin, really.

Enter a NUN, *carrying a syringe, medication, etc., that she places on a white cloth on the floor next to* OEDIPUS.

CHORUS

We're all in the military.—Show your card.—GO
DOWN, OLE MAN!—This is state property—Ever
since they've stripped the Generalissimo of his rank
THERE'S BEEN NO ONE LEFT HERE, WE'RE ALL
ORPHANED—This is a Texas blues ...

OEDIPUS (*had turned his head when the* NUN *entered. He turns back to* ANTIGONE, *and whispers in a puzzled, surprised tone*)

... Antigone? ...

ANTIGONE

Yes Pa

OEDIPUS (*turning back towards the* NUN, *dreamily*)

Who's that woman over there,

coming towards us? ...

SHE'S RIDING A MULE FROM ETNA! ... A

GREAT THESSALIAN

HAT SHIELDS HER FROM THE SUN! ... Ah,

I hope I'm not mistaken ... She's signalling ... Ah!

(*Happily*)

I recognize her! ...

NUN (*confident, bustling around him and giving a quick wink to* ANTIGONE *so she will connive in the merciful deception of the old man*)

That's right! Of course! We do

know each other!

Meanwhile she shakes the thermometer down, slips it under OEDIPUS' *shirt after loosening the strap from his arms, etc.*

OEDIPUS (*continuing as above*)

... I recognize her! Antigone? is it not her? Is

that not your elder sister

my little elder girl, my

Ismene? ...

NUN (*as above, nodding hurriedly at* ANTIGONE *with a warning, knowing half smile, and speaking in her natural voice with only a hint of exaggeration*)
Yes, yes, it is me! here I am! it's really your
daughter Ismene!
here I am!

OEDIPUS
Oh yes, I can recognize your voice as well ...
What news?

NUN (*as above*)
All good news, rest assured!
All good news!
All is well with the family! And everyone
remembers you,
everyone's waiting for you at home, as soon
as we've got you back
in good health ...

OEDIPUS
Why do you lie to an old man? You know my
sickness
has no cure.

Meanwhile the NUN *has taken the thermometer and, considering its reading, shakes her head with resigned commiseration.*

ANTIGONE (*whispering as she pulls* NUN *by the sleeve*)
What's it saying
the tremblometer? 'as 'e got a high feverish? 'as 'e?
'Scuse me, sister ... what's it saying, eh?! ...

NUN (*elusive and hypocritical, in an overly jolly tone meant to distract and appease* OEDIPUS)
Getting better . . . yes, better already . . . we must always trust in Our Lord . . . in His good assistance . . .

Starts flicking the syringe, massaging OEDIPUS' *arm for the injection, etc.*

CHORUS
By order of the Generalissimo all figures are to be redone in Roman numerals—Good morning how's it going?—This card's expired.—I spat out a lucky red ribbon, length two metres forty.—Good morning how's it going?—There's been no one left here, we're all orphaned—Ow . . . ooowww . . .
WILL I RIPEN AGAIN INTO AN EAR OF CORN?
WILL I SEED MYSELF LIKE WHEAT AGAIN?

OEDIPUS (*beginning to thrash around again*)
It's this sun, infecting the dormitories . . . Always there, nailed
to the skull of the sky... It's HIM reduced the cities to plague houses . . .
Always nailed inside this little skull . . .
All he does is stalk me . . . His machines follow me wherever I go . . .

NUN (*with authority*)
Calm down now, calm down . . .

(*Coaxing and encouraging, injecting the liquid into his vein*)

Now with a little bit of this medicine
you'll feel better
in no time . . . you'll see . . .

OEDIPUS

And the little girl—where is she?

ANTIGONE

I'm right here by your side Pa, I'm
right here . . .

OEDIPUS (*anxiously*)

Turn around!
It's shameful! I don't want you to see!

NUN

Don't worry. She did turn around!
She did! She didn't see a thing!

OEDIPUS

And that medicine you've brought me yourself—
    is it the good one?
the right one, the restful one?

NUN (*in the honeyed tone reserved for madmen or
children*)

Of course it is! Now in no time
you can have a nice sleep, you'll see . . . There, all
                        done, everything's fine,
our daddy's going to have a nice little sleep now,
                        because he was very good
and took the nice medicine that does him good . . .

OEDIPUS

I want the real one!
The one *I* mean!
Not this one . . . !

NUN

What's that? Are you saying you don't trust
me now? of course
this one I gave you is the good
medicine, the one that does you good . . .

OEDIPUS (*furiously, with senile peevishness*)

I don't believe you!
It's the same dirty old water—no use whatsoever!
Always hoodwinked!
Even if it does send me off for a bit, this sleep, in
                              sleep, has no duration,
and I'm straight back in the same old daytime
                              without beginning or end!
I want the other medicine! the forbidden one!
        The doctors stole it from me out of envy
and you're in cahoots with the doctors. All in
                                              cahoots
leaving many a lazarus to fight death outside the
                                              house gate . . .
It was my stuff, that was! I want it back! Where
                              have you stashed it?

(*Raging, drenched in sweat*)

Or have you thrown it out?!
Go away! Go!

NUN (*sweetly, securing the straps back on his arm*)
Of course not . . . fancy that . . .
calm down now . . . there . . . down . . . You'll see!
in no time at all now
you're going to have a nice little rest . . .
you'll see . . .

OEDIPUS (*whispering, trying to reach the* NUN *'s ear*)
Why don't you bring it to me, that medicine, the
restful one . . .

NUN
All right, I will . . . if you calm down,
I will . . .

OEDIPUS
Promise?

NUN
All right, yes I promise . . .

OEDIPUS (*lying back, calmer, dreamily*)
. . . This road,
what is it called?

NUN
. . . Saint Rosalie's
Rise . . .

She tiptoes toward the door. ANTIGONE, *looking worried,
leaps up and stops her.*

ANTIGONE
'Scuse, sister,

could we like—insist so 'e starts eating some-
                              thing? at least
some little soup like? cos you know, the worst
                        wiv 'im is this eating thing
'e never wants to eat but
then 'e's gonna end up all weak like—how will 'e
                        keep 'imself going?
you know 'e ain't touched a thing in thirsty-six
     hours nearly . . . even that little mouthful
                              'e took yesterday
'e couldn't keep it down . . .

NUN

   What are you carrying on for? What do you know?
   Leave it with those in charge. For now, seeing the
                                             state
   he's in, your father is going to be fed
                              intravenously.

ANTIGONE (*warily*)
   Intrav . . . is it . . . like . . . good stuff?

NUN (*hurriedly, about to exit*)
   'Course it is!

ANTIGONE (*stubbornly, almost desperately*)
   It's got some substance, yes?

NUN

   Shhh . . . I've no time now. We'll talk about it
   in an hour or so, when I come back,
                        after the service.

ANTIGONE

'Ere—I've got a letter
of recommendation for 'im!

She pulls the famous sheet out of her sleeve, and the NUN,
on her way out, stuffs it hurriedly into her apron pocket.
ANTIGONE *returns to her place by* OEDIPUS' *side. Meanwhile,*
the THREE WARDERS *have returned to their original position,*
lined up on the bench.

CHORUS

WILL I SEED MYSELF AGAIN? SHOOT FORTH
AGAIN

LIKE A FLOWER?

OEDIPUS

. . . Ah, Saint
Rosalie's Rise . . . I remember . . . it used to be
open countryside . . . then they filled that
dip in the road
with the shacks of the Town Kennels
where the reject no man's mutts are massed up
on the eve
of elimination. Ah, I see—it's them,
this howling baying chorus following me
here, relentlessly, with the sun.
Just as my eye and my hearing were given to me,
so smell
is given to them FOR FEAR. (Hope
is nothing but an alibi of fear.)
They can already smell the imminent end

of a fear with no remission or explanation
and bark to commend themselves
to nobody.

(*Tentatively beginning to sing as above*)

They too, now, over there, are a point of suffering.
And even this minimal imperceptible point of
                                    suffering
is yet another unfathomable unit
added to increase the sum total of all suffering
the fantastic and impossible sum total, that has
                                    more figures
than all bodies and all stars put together have
                                    atoms!
. . . perhaps
whosoever could reckon them all backwards,
all the way down to zero, might then
enter anew the night of Eden . . .
perhaps
the night of Eden might be entered anew
by whomsoever could reckon them all backwards
all the way down to zero . . .

CHORUS
. . . whosoever could count them all backwards
    all the way down to zero
might perhaps . . .
Owhaow . . . Owww . . .

OEDIPUS
. . . Ow . . . owww . . .

(Almost to himself)

> ... Here they go again, with their filthy
> lamentation, their idiotic psalms ...

*(Taking a judicious and curiously wayward tone, as one
passing judgment in a dream)*

> No sound
> is more hideous than human voices
> when they're devoid of nature and reason.

CHORUS
> ... No sound
> is uglier no sound ...

OEDIPUS
> Owhaaowww ... Owhaaowww ...

CHORUS *(riotously, louder)*
> Owhaaaowww ... owhaa ...

The FIRST WARDER *stands on the bench to spy through the
fanlight.*

OEDIPUS
> Owhaaowww ... owhaowww ... here they go
>   again ...

(Starting)

> WHERE AM I?!
> Why these screams? ... Someone's panting, in
>   the next room ...
> Is it a fight!? Watch out, they've got knives, nails

hidden away . . .

Who fell over? . . .

ANTIGONE

There's no one fell over, Pa
you know this bang you heard against the wall
was just some lorry braking
down in the road like—there's nobody
screaming, Pa, all those voices you hear it's just
cos of the feverish
innit Pa.

SECOND WARDER (*quietly but audibly, to the one next to him, pointing to* OEDIPUS)
What's this one
doing then? Is he ever going to die?!

Meanwhile the CHORUS *has raised a great din of laughter. The* FIRST WARDER *gets off the bench signalling to the* SECOND WARDER, *and they disappear together for a short interval.*

OEDIPUS (*thrashing around, resumes his lamentation*)
Owhaaowww . . . ow . . .

CHORUS (*in a din of laughter, as above*)
This is a military zone—Stop and you're lost—This
year the fashionable colour for straitjackets is flag red
. . . —We are all in the military—Next Monday I bought
a lucky ribbon—TB was the ruination—We are all
in the military!—One moment one moment one
moment may I breathe? thank you—Ha ha ha ha! This
is Cloud Cuckoo Land—

IT'S READY
THIS LITTLE DRESS WOVEN BY THE NUNS . . .

OEDIPUS (*thrashing around*)
   I'll never do enough time for all those lights! It's
                        HIM . . . what is he called? The
   SAINTOFSAINTS—The *NAME*—the *STATUE* . . .
   It's *HIM*, hexing me, putting machines into
                                            brains
   and drugs that won't send you to sleep into
                                            syringes . . .
   It's HIM grabbed me by the feet . . .
   The day I blinded myself with nails, I thought I
                        was putting his star out
   but instead I've immured it with myself
   inside this burial.
   The lights were too many, I'll never do enough
                        time for them.
   It's *HIM* . . . what's his name? *THELA* . . . the
                                CRIPPLE . . .
   It's *HIM* had me shadowed . . . It's *HIM* created me!
   I'd printed false papers for myself . . . what use was
                        that?
   It's *HIM*
   put the secret police on my track!
   He knows the technique . . .
   And he's always changing . . . he's a master
                        shape-shifter!
   He's changing . . . always changing! now
   he's a lamed mongrel dog . . . a bleeding lamb . . .

He's a spider multiplying inside the eye of a fly! . . .
He's a wire mesh . . . He's
a cage of bones, too narrow for my soul!

CHORUS (*laughing loudly*)
IT'S READY
THIS ROBE WOVEN BY THE FURIES
ENVELOPING ME
AND CLINGING TO ME WITH ITS THREADS!

OEDIPUS (*continuing as above*)
. . . But I can recognize him
under all his disguises! He's the RADIANT ONE,
it's HIM,
the same has held sway over me ever since the
beginning.
. . . I'll never do enough time to atone for all the
colours and lights
I'd fashioned for myself under HIS KINGDOM
like a gift promised by HIS KINGDOM . . .

CHORUS (*cheering, like a rabble riotously greeting a tribune*)
Oe-dipus!
Oe-dipus!
OE-DIPUS!

OEDIPUS (*declaiming intently*)
All my numberless births
have been under his kingdom. And from one to
the other, it's for HIM
that I've been incarnated into this last species of
suffering.

Ever since my first childhoods
when my body was a thread of aquatic alga
or a drop inside a shell,
there stirred inside me an *OTHER* anxiety,
                          searching for *HIM*!
and this stirring became an insect's antenna,
a tentacle: a first nerve of the suffering
that cannot be severed!
        From the crown of the sea anemone
        to the least moan of the mountebank toad
        to the exultant quiver
        of the airy little skeleton springing open into
                          wings and feathers
        for the mad backwards fall into the chasm of
                          the sky,
        I don't know how many strange forms of
                          limbs and tongues
        my desperate toiling took so as to grow
                          towards *HIM*:
        ever-labouring genesis, where suffering
        ferments into grains and honeys and embers
                          to be transformed
        and made blood.

CHORUS (*through manic, triumphant laughter*)
    IT'S READY! IT'S READY, THIS
    MORTUARY ROBE! HERE IT IS, GLUED TO ME,
    HOOKED ONTO MY LUNGS AND GNAWING
    WITH ITS TOOTHED THREADS!
    THE WHOLE BODY BURNS

IN THE GRIP OF THIS THING
WITH NO NAME!

Meanwhile the two absent warders have returned to their
seats on the bench, near the THIRD WARDER.

OEDIPUS (*crooning to himself*)
    . . . And today my parasite, memory
    resumes its pulsing from its fabulous lethargies.
    Like a barbaric maidservant lulling a spoilt sick
                            child, it sings once again
    the rhyme
    of my prehistories . . . Before I was born in blood
    the last season of my cycle was
    a poor VEGETAL summer . . .
    I was stuck in the soil like a damned soul,
    four feet tall if that.
    I had ALL senses, and all of my senses in one,
    and all in each of my leaves . . . My humour
                            flowing
    saline, still unripe . . . I was I was a TREE
    in its growing season . . . I was I was I was
    a little fruit tree of ordinary species . . .

CHORUS (*celebrating, like a court of miracles in a puppet*
    show)
    A tree—a little tree—a tree
    a little tree—a little tree—a little tree!
    A
    little tree!

ANTIGONE (*getting curious*)
   . . . and THEN what
   Pa?
   What happened?

OEDIPUS (*intoning a sort of* recitativo arioso *on an absurd register of liveliness and health*)
   I was a dwarf olive tree the Ionian winds bred by
                                                   chance
   on a deserted coast between the Orient and Greece,
   alone and common as an orphan.
   And grew up half wild, stretching up towards
                                                   HIM
   from my skinny little trunk, with my branches
                                       crooked by puberty
   and my dusty silvery-white tufts,
   always uncertain whether I should brag or be
                                       ashamed of myself
   since I didn't know whether I looked good or
                                             ugly, or even
   whether I was a virgin girl or a youth! All my
                               nights were troubled
   with expectation of the morning, when HE
   would return with his kisses and caresses.
                               Thoughtless, careless
   kisses and caresses, of course, since like some
                                       wondrous whore
   HE would give them away to any and everyone
   without ever tarnishing even the least scale of his
                       golden body, his golden fur, his golden
                                             fingernails.

But I never wondered about HIM: not even who
                                    HE might be
perhaps I thought HIM an animal.
And my desperate lovesick pubescence
was wringing my unripe roots with the yearning
to break the vice grip of the earth.
All along the limbs branching out from me
in the gawkiness of my hungry development
my still-childish muscles
quivered so hard in a lust for animal running
they were almost pawing the ground.
And the restless lymph burst out of my bark
in lacerations and rashes like burns,
mottling my bitter little fruits
with a bloodlike colour. It was HIM
who from the summery autumnal sky
fired me to the extraordinary adventure
lashing me with his burning whips and bathing
            me in his honeyed saliva and his radiant
                                    seed!
and when, a feral, trembling little beast, I finally
                    tore free of my vegetal bark,
HE gathered me up in his divine hand, warm as
                    motherly flesh and ringed
            with all the splendours of earth's mines!
And to HIM
did I address my first voice: ejaculating such love
as to sound like a howl of haggard restraint.

        And so I found myself alone in my nativity
abandoned to the deafening lull of the underwood

and the poor wrinkled udders of goats.
Moved by HIS star, the baptismal angels had
already
descended to pierce my feet with a spike
as with the animal marked for the offering. And
ever since
I have been left with this impeded foot.
I was a hybrid
with goat-like curls and carnivorous little teeth
and I had the merriment of the hunt: for in each
and every blood
I was made to recognize HIM: colour and flavour.
HE was certainly male like myself. A slicker who
bloodies the moons and leaves them with
open veins.
A hybrid himself even, perhaps?
A cross between a red-striped tiger and a vulture
with orange and yellow feathers
devouring the living and the dead.
A childish cannibal gobbling up all the stars in
the morning.
Perhaps my goatish curly-lock face
my brown eyes and fanned-out hands
are stamped with his emblem?
Ah, bitter distance! joyful agnation!
I knew not HIS name, but HE knew mine . . .
Breathlessly I rushed after his call.
And it was in the attempt to reach HIM
that I launched into the first crippled run
of my poor injured little feet.

It was the yearning for his name made my tongue
speak.
HE was playing tag
calling me: 'Oedipus! hey, macho! king Oedipus!
hey!' From anywhere, in his multifarious
tongues:
'Oedipus!' From the bottom of a puddle, from
inside a walnut: 'Oedipus!'
In a swarm of gnats or in a scale: 'Oedipus! hey,
darkie!' In the odour of
a decomposed corpse,
of a rotting bunch of grapes. In the rings of some
smoke: 'Oedipus! Swellfoot!
hey!'
In the terrible din of my pulsing ribcage: 'Oedipus!
King Oedipus!'
And it was to see his worshipped body that I
raised my head.
And named HIM! but in a prayer
as a subject might name the king of kings.
And HE replied by way of a song
telling me that I was the deformed bastard
the ugly freak of nature
and I'd have been better off
never born.

CHORUS (*laughing as above*)
HERE IT COMES AGAIN
THE FEROCIOUS UNBEARABLE SICKNESS, HERE
IT COMES

STRIKING AGAIN! HERE IT IS
GLUED TO ME, DIGGING RIGHT INTO MY RIBS,
CLINGING TO MY

AIRWAYS AND
GNAWING . . .

OEDIPUS (*continuing as above*)
. . . And in vain, at the end of his song, frightened
as an animal,
leaping up and down across the slopes of that
rugged underwood, glancing
askance at the golden curve of the air,
did I wait for another word from him, at least
one last word! that would do as a reassuring
explanation
for my trusting and bewildered heart.
But in his final silence,
I was caught in slumbering stupors, and fell back
down on my knees
in a huge shuddering.
Once again that amphibious temptation, blindly
yearning for him
through all my births like a fantastic
ever unripe root,
came to stir every cell in my body, usurping my
will that stretched out towards HIM
with the instinct of sunflowers.
And with my mind barely knowing
my tongue moved in stutters to spell out for HIM
my first

prayer
of adoration:

    'O e-ter-nal love
    st-ar of st-ars
    praise be to you, for the ab-surd mir-age masks
                            that you wear
    to cover your un-fathomable beauty
    and for the count-erfeit titles and pseudonyms
                            you take to hide
    your un-named maj-esty.
    O alibi and contrad-iction
    mys-tery of mysteries
    you who give yourself through de-nial and teach
                triumph through hu-mil-iation,
    who will comprehend your tragic jargon?
    you send ciphered messages, from king to king
    so that your se-cret al-liance will be recognized
    only by those who can read your un-conveyable
    and dif-ficult
            signs . . .
    O fabulous
    ambiguity! . . .
    Blessed is the seraphim angel you stir with the
                      anguish of the Gehenna
    and the peace-loving man you provoke to a brawl
             with your thuggish call: 'I'll see you on the
                                street!'
    Blessed is the mummy's boy you kick out into the
                                  fray
    and the lover who leaves his dear warm den

when your mobs whistle by at nightfall
and the beginner trapezist who at the sound of
                    your fanfare plunges into
'the deadly
triple mid-air somersault'!
Ah blessed is the one who turns hoodlum for you
and infringes your official orders to heed your
                    clandestine command
O heavenly hoax.
I render thanks unto you for your song
now unfolding before me in its duplicity and its
                    shining favour,
like certain horrific dreams that turn out to be
                    heavenly flares
sent to spotlight the malison
before the trap springs.
O holy holy holy!
You
have denounced to this my self its own
                    pitiful infamy
because you want to return me to my other
Self! to that future once promised by the mysteries
and anticipated by yourself when, in our
                    common merriment,
you would jokingly call me: King Oedipus!
'Jokingly' . . . ? . . . ? . . . I recognize you!
    I recognize you
O jealous sharing of secrets!
And in your silence I again sing to myself all alone
your song d e c i p h e r e d ! ! Here it is:

THIS MY SELF
REJECTED BY HEAVEN, THIS
DEFORMED LITTLE SQUIRT OF A BASTARD
IS NOTHING BUT THE UGLY DEGRADED
                              FLIPSIDE
OF MY REAL SELF: K I N G OEDIPUS!
AND I'D BE BETTER OFF UNBORN RATHER
                        THAN LIVING OUT
THIS ACCURSED BETRAYAL.
A N D Y E T
IF I SHUN THIS ALIEN NEST, THIS FERAL
                              FAMILY,
AND START MY SEARCH, CHANCES ARE
I CAN FIND IT, THAT INCREDIBLE
REAL
MYSELF . . .

                                        . . .

that luminous Double of mine, your beloved
your like!
Golden as your eyelashes
deep blue as your room.
Male and female like you,
O hermaphrodite love! and mother and father,
O only star! you who invent the measureless
                                        creation!
In your name, Ayin,
under the guidance of your comets and zodiac fires,
I want to find it again.
I'll live like a bandit,

I'll go begging,
sell myself as merchandise in brothels,
I'll be a monk, a guerrilla
and a pirate,
only to find it again.
Unto you be rendered all praise and all
                    thanksgiving
for this trial you now set upon me, no matter its
                    harshness and toil.
And for each of my braveries and conquests
          leading up to the wonderful prize,
glory to you!
glory!
glory!'

And so, with no farewells,
wearing only my dirty overalls—and with my
                    little flick knife

as only luggage,
I found myself fully ready
for the great escape.

CHORUS
   Away!
   Walk walk walk you bravest little soldier
   you illiterate little prince, killer cool dude.
   Fly fly fly
   you swarthy little pheasant, lamed little
                    mountain cockerel,
   you raving swarm, Verb, magic philtre, rocket,
                    sweet vulnerable fauna,

hundred-thousand-revs engine, bandolero, night
owl,
fly and fly.
On all the routes in the school atlas
and the adventurer's,
Caribbean Philippines Beverly Hills
Great Urals Monte Carlo Jerusalem
and where Sitting Bull mumbles and rumbles
and thunders
and where Pinocchio sows his gold sequins in
the soil
and where Diabolik shakes on it with Batman
and where Saint Michael rides amid bells and
leaves
fly
fly Lambretta fly Peyote
among the Tartars and the Malays
the Eskimos and Moroccans
and Egyptians
set sail with the crusader ship
the Britannic steamship the atomic mushroom
the Olympic chariot
and riding a she-ass
and three hundred dromedaries
ride and roam roam and ride
lightning furlana gymkhana ultrasound
unique and crazy adventure
brave Oedipus
run
in search of your own shining flesh

to finally double into your own unique body
a king's body,
the only body that's worthy of death.
Run run fly to that ultimate orgasm—howl of *the*
                    unparalleled sweetness—
sigh of health regained after the delirious sickness
of carnal separation.
Through north winds and siroccos
to the Kremlin and Mecca in Atlantic caves and
                                lunar mines
and Thule and Cimmeria
jump and crawl, Swellfoot!
search for him
the fugitive unrecognizable lookalike
the angel with the blue-white eye and the winged
                        ankles
the boy with wind for his shoes.

OEDIPUS

In the Upanishads and the Kabbala
in the blues and agitprop
and in numbers and quanta and proverbs and
                    comic strips and magic flutes
from the Place-of-a-Skull to Tenochtitlan and from
Menelik's palace to the White Horse
                    Tavern
and in jailhouses and dance houses on film sets
                and boxing rings and night clubs
and among doctors, militiamen and assassins
and in the rubble and marshes and death camps,

all around the world all around the

anti-world

to search for my treasure the wedding ring lost

in the stream
the wafer from the defaced altar
the bloodied rib of laceration.

OEDIPUS
Even at the cost of walking three thousand years
I was almost certain I'd find him,
my beloved. And so
in the mirth of my free adventure independent of
any itineraries open to inexhaustible chance
humming and whistling
I set off.

Little did I know
that all my roads—main roads or through roads
or shortcuts or detours—
had already been traced out by HIM
in his preordained geometry.
Each step I took was calculated. Each movement,
manoeuvred by his minions.
My victorious trials were nothing but fakes
concocted to deceive me!
The Sphynx, a bribed procuress. The whole game
stacked in advance.
And my departure might be said to be a
consequence of the arrival

or vice versa
since the arms of the cross meet at a certain point
even from infinity
and that fixed point
is the room assigned by HIM in the beginning
                              that equals the end.
In truth, my first prayer of adoration
     must have meant nothing to HIM,
same as the monotone of a frog or a donkey foal.
Just as HIS ancient voices
of games and calls—and that very last, hideous
                              song of his—
must have been nothing more
than echolike phenomena and hallucinations
from my own nerves. For HE—unlike those we call
'the dead'—
does abide in the fabulous timespans of death:
                              blind, there
amid the huge light of the stellar graveyard,
unscathed from the incurable wound of mothers,
a deaf mute.
     And here I am now, strapped to his cross
so that my veins are wrung into the veins of this
                              wood
and at times I think I'm turning double, we're
                              twain in one
I—HIM.
Except HE, unborn, shines impassive in the
                    affirmation of his eternal death,
while I burn in my desperate denial. O night

night, my blissful home, night my first milk
                              my sweetness, why
do you not return to console me? for only one
                              night? You mercy, you rest,
come help me. JOCASTA!!
Jocasta you
help me
Mamma!!

VOICE FROM OUTSIDE (*a bully's voice, in rude health*)
Ah! ah! ah!
he wants his mamma now
our thug, our hoodlum, our hooligan!
our HERO!
ah! ah!
he wants his mamma!

VOICE *fades out.*

CHORUS (*in gales of gross laughter as above*)
AND HERE I AM AGAIN
HERE IN THE VICE GRIP OF THIS RAGING
    INSATIABLE SICKNESS
THAT QUELLS ITS HUNGER ON ME, AND
    WON'T LET GO!
YOU MUST ALL LOOK AT IT, THIS BODY OF
    MISERY! OH
MY HANDS, MY ARMS, EQUAL TO THE TOILS
    OF GIANTS! HERE I AM
UNDONE BY A DISASTER BEYOND MY SENSES,
REDUCED TO HOWLING . . .

ANTIGONE

Pa!!

Don't cry like that please Father, my heart's
    breaking in two just to look at your tears
                            of blood
Father, I'd give the sight from my two eyes to see
                    you happy again Pa
but you must cheer up Pa the hard times'll be over
and soon you'll be all right again
another couple of days & you'll be just fine
and as for me—don't doubt me dear Pa, I'll always
                    be here by your side
and even if you don't get your sight back never
        mind! there's nothing much to see anyway
and then when something good comes along I can
                    always tell you can't I
when there's something that is
good to see.

OEDIPUS

Why

do you call me Father? No man is father to
                    another. We are all born
of one and the same mother. I don't want
to be called Father. I want to forget
that name . . .

ANTIGONE

All right Pa it's all right Pa it's as you say Pa . . .

OEDIPUS

And now pay attention, you must pray with me.
    Repeat
after me: 'O Holy
Ladies, O Blissful Mothers,
O Merciful Furies . . . '

ANTIGONE

O Holy Ladies
O Blissful Mothers . . .

OEDIPUS

' . . . O Merciful Furies!
You who accompany Oedipus on his automaton's
                                                    way
scattering him like sand in your fantastic fluttering,
you, through the angelic aberration of mercy,
                        reverse this rush, take me back.
Let me find again the little wayside den
that hides the heavenly child whose forehead's
            marked with the two crosses, the kid goat
                            with deformed feet
and there, as had been promised, let us fell him,
            the bastard, barely dewed with his own
                                first tears,
before his comical off-key question
rises to outrage the secrets
of the radiant throne.
His newborn blood will be offered in sacrifice to
                the radiant spectre—Phoebus—
or Ra—or Yahweh—or Coatl—or whomsoever

might want to be that name.
And then the sweet solar rain of the equinox
will fall in forgiveness '*ah, I was created!*' on his
cloven little heart
to seed the wondrous cactus
that leads to the nocturnal consolations when it's
drunk.
It is said that this fruit is one of the mysteries
buried in the decayed garden.
That Janardhana, the shining charioteer, gave
some to the boy Arjuna.
That the lily of the Annunciation was one of its
flowers.
That the Magi brought one of its seeds (the fourth,
hidden gift).
That Socrates, Memory-of-Archangels, drank a
drop with his hemlock
laughing in the multiple bliss of his subversive
death.
That Milarepa's luminous shadow whispered its
secret in the ear
of Rechung, the evangelist, his dearest one . . .
etcetera, etcetera.
Of course these are all barbaric rumours and
poppycock.
But then I believe in barbarians' chatter and
childish fibs.
I believe in the Minotaur and the Hydra and the
Chimera and the Booted Puss
and in the wandering Jew and in Cagliostro

                              winking from the moon
            and in the conversations of Mohammed with
                                              Gabriel
            the hundred baskets of Cana and the blood
                                sweated in the olive garden
            and in the speaking statue
            and in the forest of suicides

CHORUS

    I believe in the fibs of wet nurses in fairies and
                                          ogresses
    in ghosts and in demons and in all the ranks
                                      of angels
    in the writing of lightning and the voices of
                                          thunder

OEDIPUS

    I believe in ignorance and dreams and delirium
    I believe in all the most prodigious or idolatrous
                                          stories
    and in all impossible things.
    Only death, my own death,
    I cannot believe in.
    O Holy Mothers of fear
    you who return to fabulous anarchy
    the corrupted visions of the temporal order,
    console me at least with your little death.
    I believe in you.
    I pray to you.
    Listen to me.'

        . . . Antigone!! where are you?? Antigone? . . .

ANTIGONE

Yes Pa

I'm right here beside you Pa don't worry about a
thing cos I'm always right here by your side
you know you mustn't believe all those nasty
impressions that scare you Pa, they're
nothing really, it's just the
feverish innit
cos the feverish, that's what's got you living in a
dream like . . .

Pa

I'm going to sponge your face down with some
nice cool water now—and your hair too,
so you get a bit of relief.

*She proceeds, wetting his lips and the roots of his hair with
water from the bottle.*

OEDIPUS

. . . WHERE are we? . . .

ANTIGONE

We are
. . . we're at home!
Pa!
We're upstairs in the room in our house in the
evening . . . it'll be about
seven o'clock—quarter past maybe . . .

OEDIPUS (*without hearing her*)

. . . where are we? . . .
. . . don't go . . . My sickness is unbearable.

Someone give me some remedy, no matter if
temporary, to interrupt the nagging numbering
of this incalculable day without an end
and entirely counted out already!
Any other state, as long as it's other, would be a
                                        rest for me.
One night is all I ask for, one night at least. Just a
                                        break, a rest.
    ... I'm thirsty ...

(ANTIGONE *is quick with the glass of water, but he pushes it
away roughly. Then he suddenly breaks into song, with the
hoarse and insane voice of an old drunk, his head lolling
from side to side.*)

When I was coming home from Ethio-piah
with a bagful of talers alalà
I was so black in the face
they called me *the Abyssinian* ah ah
ah ah the Abyssinian, Lamey and Swellfoot
what a nice lot what a good old bunch ...

CHORUS
What a nice lot what a good old bunch
tra la la.

OEDIPUS (*with a corporal's authority*)
STEP IN TIME, STICK TO THE RHYTHM.

The neon light above the door starts fading. And the NUN
*returns, but in the faint light she looks much taller, almost
gigantic. As she passes through, she gestures with her chin*

to the THREE WARDERS, *who exit in a line. The rustle of her gown with its huge folds—and the whisper of the ample starched wings of her headdress—have a strange sonority, as if perceived through an unnaturally sharpened sense of hearing.*

NUN
　Shhh . . .

Bends towards OEDIPUS.

OEDIPUS
　I'm thirsty . . . I'm thirsty . . .

CHORUS
　GIVE DRINK TO THE THIRSTY AND TO THOSE
　　　　　　　　　　　　　　WHO SUFFER
　AND HAVE A BITTER HEART.
　GIVE DRINK TO THE THIRSTY AND TO THOSE
　　　　　　　　　　　　　　WHO SUFFER AND
　HAVE A
　BITTER HEART.
　　MAY THEY DRINK
　AND FORGET THEIR MISERY
　AND NO LONGER HAVE
　ANY MEMORY OF THEIR TOIL.

After this, for the first time in the whole evening, the CHORUS *is silent.*

OEDIPUS
　. . . I'm thirsty . . .
　. . . Who are you? . . .

NUN
Shhh . . .

OEDIPUS (*secretively, anxiously*)
And the medicine
—did you bring it me?

The NUN *nods, as does her huge magnified shadow on the wall.*

OEDIPUS
Which
medicine

NUN (*laughing benevolently, with the aged voice of a mad-woman*)
That one!
That one!

OEDIPUS
I remember your laugh. You were laughing like that
the last time I heard you.
So it's you?

NUN (*as above*)
It's me
and it isn't me.

OEDIPUS
Did you really bring it? Did you really
have mercy on me?

NUN (*as above*)
Always the same, you: always suspicious.
Just drink it, and you'll surely
recognize the taste . . .

OEDIPUS

I cannot tell things apart by their taste.
By now, anything I eat or drink has the
same dirty old flavour for me . . .

NUN (*as above*)

How can you even think I would lie to you?
Who gave you water when you first were thirsty?
And why else would I have been waiting for you,
here at the P. H.
until you came tonight?

OEDIPUS

But why did you dress up
as a Medieval Empress?

NUN (*as above*)

An empress!! Fancy that! Always the same,
you: always fanciful.
Fanciful, and a reader. Too many books.
But luckily, one little sign of the cross
will rub all of those books right out.
An empress I am
and I'm not. Some see it one way, some the other.
. . . Here, lean on my arm . . . Have you forgotten
the story of the giant that slips
through the magic little ring? . . . Here, drink up,
my pretty little 'un.
Drink up.

(As OEDIPUS *juts his lips out to drink, she starts singing to
him in her laughing, hoarse, madwoman's voice and in the
coaxing tone of nursery rhymes and lullabies:*)

There was a giant called Sacripiant who was
     bigger than St Peter's dome.
The ring is small, won't fit at all, and he must pass
     through to get home.
But the little ring that was a magic thing
turned him into a flying flea.
And the giant Sacripiant
slipped through easier than Hail Maree!

Drink up now.
Drink up.

OEDIPUS
     Ah how
     sweet it is.

NUN
     Shhh . . .

In the silence, the only sound is OEDIPUS *gulping, avid and inno-
cent as a nursling. Meanwhile, the light keeps fading. Sated,*
OEDIPUS *lays his head back on the pillow.*

CHORUS (*singing*)
     HEAVEN AND EARTH HAVE RANSOMED ME.
               PLANTS HAVE DELIVERED ME
     FROM THE DEATHS THROUGH SOMA, THEIR
                                   KING.

The NUN *tiptoes away, down the narrow staircase. As soon as
she's gone,* ANTIGONE *approaches* OEDIPUS *with a sly expres-
sion, and quickly busies herself loosening the straps around his
arms.*

ANTIGONE (*whispering, complicitous*)
> Cos there's no one here on the night shift innit
> they's sure to be much less watching like
> at least with your arms free
> you're gonna sleep a bit better
> innit Pa

(*Her feat accomplished, she lifts his two hands, gently shaking them to alert him to the advantages of his new situation. In an almost festive tone:*)

> Look Pa
> much betterer now
> with your arms a bit looser
> innit Pa?

OEDIPUS (*lets his hands flop back onto the sheet. Smiling*)
> Mercifully, by now,
> my arms
> are no longer any use to me.

The neon light is down to little more than a glimmer, and through the fanlights comes barely a faint glow like that of dying embers. At the bottom of the stairwell, little coloured lights begin to move, as on a carousel or a Christmas tree, accompanied by childish laughter like the screeching of small feral beasts. Through this laughter, we begin to make out three treble voices (one soft, one clearer and the third rather nasal), alternating or chorusing in a sort of discordant serenade.

VOICES
> Ad-iter dakso aj-ayata

            aj-ayata aj-ayata,
        dak-sa u
            u u u u u
        ad-itih pa-ri aditih tih tih tih tih pa-
            ri!

OEDIPUS *laughs.*

VOICES
    Oedipus!
        Oedipus!
                Oedipus!
    Oedipus!   Oedipus!
                Oedipus!

OEDIPUS
    Who's
    calling me?

VOICES
            It is us! the three fairies of this place!
        The Benign Ones worshipped in these
            underground shrines!
        your companions of the velvet foot
        and wild pelt made of eyes and vibratile hair!
        Of all your supplications and prayers we under-
                                stood nothing
        but as it was written
        it is here in our abode that you will now sing
        the Angelus of the evening, descending
        the stairway of the seven gates.

OEDIPUS

I will never
sing again.

VOICES

You *will* sing

sing

sing   sing   sing   and
sing AGAIN . . .

CHORUS (*in the stupefied voices of sleepers*)
. . . Here.   —   Here.   —   Here opens
the coloured stairway of the seven gates!

VOICES

At each gate you must surrender one degree
of the radiant spectrum

CHORUS (*as above*)
And in exchange the gate will open. Seven
degradations and seven farewells
are the price of my passage.

VOICES

The male body of the beloved was a feast of seven
splendours.

CHORUS (*as above*)
All its gates will once again be closed over me.
. . . here I am, a blind man at the ramp.

VOICES (*exalted*)
The FIRST ONE
is the GREEN gate!

OEDIPUS (*singing, in a charmed voice, almost sleeping already*)
Green. The returns!
I am the swallow's pupils, measures of a needle's eye
in which the whole heavenly glass pane of the
return is thrown wide open,
with fields of wheat, and the coloured shadows
the wind makes among flower stems
changing with every instant, no two ever alike;
and all the numberless grass blades,
and on each grass blade each tiny seedling of
wheat in bud,
no two ever the same.

VOICES
DEEP BLUE is the colour
of the SECOND gate!

OEDIPUS
Deep blue. Home!
I am the nocturnal rhythm of the becalmed sea
on the harbour's edge,
below the precincts of the fortress where the
recruit sleeps and in his dreams
thinks himself back home with the family,
sleeping in the stables by the breath
of the mare
and the thriving foal
that he himself saw into birth last winter,
he himself its midwife.

VOICES
The THIRD gate is the colour RED!

OEDIPUS

Puberty!
I am the racing heart of the girl who trembles at
the transgressed prohibition
as she walks with the boy
on the way back from class in the evening,
and at the moment of the clandestine goodbye
                              on the doorstep
yields her mouth barely dewed with first love
to a kiss that's still cold with childhood and theft.

VOICES

The FOURTH one is the colour YELLOW!

OEDIPUS

The orisons!
I am the mist, the hundred thousand gleamings,
the fabulous seeding of early morning Orients
that rises to the windows with the first shiver,
invades the chamber, embroiders its icy
                              little shawls
for the two poor bigoted dugs frostbitten
in their little vests of raw wool, and dews
                              the eyelashes
lowered at Elevation.
And high over the incenses and flames that
                              cannot burn it
shifts with the polar current,
seeps through smog, sails with its fleet of
   a hundred thousand ships through the
                              vapours of harbours

and mixes with the smokes of Buchenwald,
                    swathing its ether gauze
around the blood of agony.
And fluffy like childhood down
settles on the statues of Olympia.

VOICES

The WHITE
gate!

OEDIPUS

HIS colour! the ONE, the crux of fire! the radiant
                                circle!
I am the cut of the buried diamond, to which the
                        stars all rush like arrows
I am the drop where all the rainbows meet!
I am the pixie of the invisible mirror, wisping
and leaping and flitting around the terrace
and the cat runs crazy after it
and the little boy laughs.

VOICES

This
is the sixth gate.
The colour black.

OEDIPUS

yes, yes,
        that's what
I wanted,
        I always wanted,
I always wanted,

> to return
> > to the body
> > > where I was born.

VOICES

And this last one is the gate to the void.

OEDIPUS

The
gate
to
the
void.

By now the corridor has fallen into total darkness. And in the darkness the CHORUS *is heard again, but all its voices are one and the same with the voice of* OEDIPUS, *multiplied and fading into the distance.*

CHORUS OF OEDIPUS' VOICE

'O sacred Being!
too long have I troubled
your divine golden quiet. Of this dark sorrow
> hidden inside life
you have learnt too much from me.
Oh, forgive and forget!
Like that cloud over the moon that shines in peace,

> > > > so

do I pass, and you rest in the serene
repose of your beauty,
O my light!'

Silence. Then the tolling of a bell. In the corridor, the lighting is back to normal, with the addition of the neon light in the stairwell. But there is no one left in the place. Curiously, the deserted corridor resounds with the multiple ticking of clocks, some near, some far. Then from the bottom of the stairs comes the weeping, howling voice of ANTIGONE.

ANTIGONE'S VOICE
Pa! Paa! Paaaa!

IV

The Yearning for Scandal

1

I am the bitter point of the oscillations
between the moons and the tides.

2

At the promised, necessary, impossible meeting
once again today I am trying for the erased frontier.
I have marked with a cross the point of bitter water.
CELA COMMENÇA PAR QUELQUES DÉGOÛTS.

Grace or perdition, the dances begin
and I am banished from all human rooms.
Like a man enslaved I delve into the buried Indias
of an Arctica of extreme splendours the night can't touch.

Uninfected by breaths, safe from the bloodied ocean
is the desert homeland with no horizon or gates.
I recognize its funerary geometries
the undecipherable ideograms where every history is
                                                atoned for.

Multiplied by the ices of a fixed rainbow
along the gleaming galleries of the spectrum
the perverted figures of the Lares are lost
in the last white fire negating all forms.

Space is denatured to fit the dimension of horror
but running the field is the law. The uprooted centre
strains towards its own lacerating rays. The body is ash.
The only point is the beating of the heart crushed
while still alive.

Help me help me sweet flavour.

3

And you rush over, echo of an echo, from our vegetal nests
predating the first barbarity, where you and I are one
neither man nor woman, a gleeful unpuberty with no history,
until they part us, to call us to their slaughter.

Having been on this side of death, we are lesser than
                                                    mortals,
but good for the game of kingdom come that elates them.
Innocent of the rage that has tied them to the wheel,
we hold the secret they forbid themselves.

Asking for the answer again and eternally denying it
is their desperate choice. And like the gypsy actors
unmasking the infamy of the usurped palace,
so are we called upon in time to stage the crime.

And me parted from you, in the bloodied tearing
of birth. The funeral suppers are laid, crosses
and scaffolds are raised, tribes gathered.
And the slain son, the mother torn apart.

So I lose you, and you lose me, in the pestilence
of this city. Deranged inside common time,
we forget our feasting nation
and our prenatal games.

Until the whimsical patience of fate

should return to the grave of chance and decipher
the interred letters to be rearranged
into our one name

and take us back to our first arboreal rooms
swings suspended this side of the current
where the harrowing mill of all hallucinations
is nothing but the turn of our airy scherzo.

We are less than human, pure
of the vice of death.

4

Yet always, called upon, we return inside the mirage
where they revolve corrupted by the drug of death.
We sit at their sordid tribal banquets
where night-time anguish gathers them together.

And with our strings and flutes, guileless primal voices,
to their question we repeat ever the same answer:

> *Night and day are one*
> *modulating passages of one and the same song.*
>
> *The only secret is: there is no secret.*
> *You have never strayed from the garden of the first day.*
> *The baseness of forms usurping it from you*
> *is nothing but a risible theatre of your mirages.*
> *It is still the first day.*
>
> *The span of your millennia*
> *was really but a little flight on our swings.*
> *Your body and mind are instruments rigged up*
> *for deformation and imposture.*
> *Your fief is intact.*
>
> *Have no fear of the night.*
> *Yield to her healing*
> *blissfully, as if this were the time before mothers, when*
> *all earthly blood is still but a vein of the sea.*
> *The breath is not your measure.*

For you, abducted in the spinning of your deformed
star,
the whole mirror of the rainbow is empty white horror.
Mirror yourselves in the point of rest,
recognize your unscathed face
the freshness of your own colours.
Your body is invulnerable.

LASS DIE GLOCKEN KLINGEN KLINGEN.

5

But, like larvae of a besieged population
fearing proffered peace more than its own slaughter,
holding fast to their rubble
they insult and refute our foreign voices.

And like hostages of an anarchy with no rank
denied the trust of ransom,
we are the prey left to their puerile revenge:
I for the wounds, and you for pity.

Unequal to the ordeal of torture and death
we two are the ultimate touchstone of their scandal.
We have to justify the value of their field
by putting our poor agony on show.

And the dream takes effect. In sweat and convulsions
we ourselves recant our own testimony.
Broken and scattered among their deathly rags
we surrender ourselves to the earth.

LULLABY LULLABY
LULLA LULLA LULLA.

6

O ambiguity, provocation of two voices in one,
you who amused death with your pretty little song,
your dust is too scant to sate death.
Their death is hungry. Their death is bored.

The angry dance of slaughter
never rests over my little stone.
But rest from time and memory is deaf.
By now even your weeping has found respite.
You too, girl, are turned to stone.
There is no answer.

At least until another genesis. Tomorrow
from a nameless orient, from a plague house a ghetto
a harlem, a baby's cry rises again.
'A boy is born.' And radiant lady you bend
your amputated smile towards me.

No one recognizes our eyes
unscathed by death.
The wings of the first day beat unfledged and lost.
The song of returning love
is but a gurgle in the throat.

For the solar feast to be consumed
the guest must arrive obscure and bare.
Perhaps he's a bastard name registered at some hospital.

Or a bundle of rags hidden in a women's dormitory
inside a barbed-wire camp.
Though the camp guards hunt for him
they will not find him.
It's not yet time.

   He must mature—but unawares.
As a diversion from the boredom of their death
he will have to innocently recite a perverted comedy
where the ultimate secret he shares
must in the end seem even to himself a tall tale and a
                                                betrayal.
He will have to recognize his own diversity like a grimace
and give himself up, as if to grace,
to their common vice
invoking blindness like a pardon.
Tomorrow
and tomorrow and tomorrow and tomorrow and tomorrow
and

   ICI VA-T-ON SIFFLER POUR L'ORAGE, ET LES
SODOMES ET LES SOLYMES, ET LES BÊTES FÉROCES ET
LES ARMÉES.

7

But this time a frozen, panting motherly voice
rushed over, echo of an echo,
as he stood faltering
over the pole of native solstices
and said to him: 'Don't be born any more. Tear each
                                              nerve loose

from the pulsing device that still nails you
to this crossroads of space rays.
And give yourself up inside the sail furling you back in
to lower you sleeping to your nest
until your wound is closed.
Heal yourself from memory. Break free
from every other tomorrow.'

OUT OUT BRIEF CANDLE.

But he fought this coaxing voice
like he would a spectral thief.
Pleading for help he tore the marine sheet
already enclosing him for rest.
And his childish voice cried out: 'I love them!
Perhaps the answer they awaited
was not as easy as my callow song.
The subject of their words is flimsy merchandise
they exchange with counterfeit coin.
I am the gold standard.

Until I have invented the words of gold
I must return to the trial.
The fault is mine.'

Ô SAISONS, Ô CHÂTEAUX!

8

So once again the child's cry is merged
with the blood's beat.
The wound's clot leavens, the circle of ice
is changed into a womb's warmth.
At the first wild light, the upturned alchemy
transmuting the substance of limbos into incarnation
unfolds equal to its other, which at the second light
resembles the wasting of death.
Here comes dissolution, the dust of rocks
crumbling to the bloodied sea
and the wondrous putrefaction of lichens
among teeming corals and the mounting of medusas
and stars moving their petals
as their antennae feel for the gleam of twilights.
On the little estuary
the saliva of foams strands in a dirge of bubbles.
A rose is born.

QUANNO MAMMETA T'HA FATTO
VO' SAPE' CHE CE METTETTE?
MIELE ZUCCHERO E CANNELLA MIELE ZUCCHERO
E CANNELLA

9

And so I'm a girl again. I recognize
the eager mouth and haggard colour
the eyes still wet with heavenly mire
the impossibility of weeping
the tender animal fist that won't let go
the glee of the naked chest under the school uniform
the thigh untainted by high summer fire
the childish incestuous belly.
The body of love is ready
for the ambiguous visitation.

And the prayer of expectancy will rise
spelt out in the processions of suburbia.
The barbaric virginal sore will mix its fevers
with the infections of the downtrodden neighbourhood.
Chiagneva sempre ca durmeva sola . . .
The mandolins
will be slaughtered in the childish grand guignol
of revolutions, assassin herbs and hungers,
when one midnight, amid adoring curses,
the star in the shape of a kite will unhitch
from the chariot of Böotes.

O teenagers, jesters of God!
Even the pirate frills of prostitution
will be but childish Sundays.

10

And the poor little tuppence bed
has turned into a mysterious island stirring awake.
She can go out alone: easy, she's invisible.
On the doorstep, just come from Africa, a little snub-
                                        nosed archangel
conspiringly whispers in her ear
a prophecy that signifies nothing.
The barely born island is still a marsh of lava.
Not long to the first day.

And with her winged feet she begins to walk
across the seething marsh, but without touching it.
In the fermenting death of the heavenly vapour
reborn as earths & moons, the rainbow stairway's mirror
is multiplied in bubbles of lava, native lymphs
of orchards and of diadems. With her playful arms she
is one of the Maias stretching
their multicoloured wedding scarves
over the restraint of the first light.

The blaze of submerged craters
burns on the eastern edges, where already
calcinated lava rises in black towers.
Sulphur pools are steaming
this side of the black ridge
steep over the shoreline's night-time chill

and—first creatures—the eucalypti
tremble still damp over the bay
until in a deafening eruption of stars
the summer day blazes alive.

Frightened of the fiery rocks erupting
from the solar crater to stone her,
she runs to the paradise of eucalypti
where through the arborescence the metamorphosis
already is unfolding into playful
new morning creatures.
THE BEASTS OF FABULOUS ELEGANCE.
The buds of tree trunks open
drowsy eyelids over their mottled eyes
and from the spring-fresh branches zodiac horns
rise up in barbaric crowns over the muzzles of bark
that soften into young down. Loosened from their trunks
the gleeful slender legs are quivering
in the sweet nodes of their muscles. And a great ringing
of forest hooves chases through the echoes like pealing bells
with a new explosion of stars.

Above her the oblong leaves of the eucalyptus
vibrate as their veins swell up and fledge
and unfold into more winged little bodies.
And the lava cliff rock evolves into the shapes
of elephants and primordial saurians, statues still imprisoned
in the formless mineral black. On the horizon
the Semite ark of the floods
slides below a double crisscrossed rainbow
past the aquatic strip of the sky.

The ground is all a luminous pubescence.
The small eucalyptus grove, a copse
hardly large enough for a child's games,
is a huge valley. She has lost
track of herself in there. She had
a straw hat and a light scarf
left under a eucalyptus tree
but eucalypti are budding crosses, all alike
through endless labyrinths. The scales and wing-cases
                                                    of light
crumble in a mist teeming with sparks
in the narcotic noontide sun. The double rainbow
has moved its wings of quivering feathers
that rustle in the daytime firmament
veering towards the island in their flight.

She laughs she laughs
because, breaking loose from a cross,
fresh-faced laughing sun-kissed
here comes towards her
the boy Adam.

11

And the fruits harvested from the twilight clouds
shall be drunk on the terrace as evening comes
when the peace of being born is celebrated
as after a victory

EN EFFET ILS FURENT ROIS TOUTE UNE MATINÉE, OÙ
LES TENTURES CARMINÉES SE RELEVÈRENT SUR LES
MAISONS, ET TOUT L'APRÈS-MIDI, OÙ ILS S'AVANCÈRENT
DU CÔTÉ DES JARDINS DES PALMES.

PART THREE
Folk Songs

I

Song Of The H.F. And The U.M.

In Three Parts

1

EXPLANATORY INTRODUCTION

? What does H.F. mean? It is an abbreviation
of *Happy Few*.
? And who are the Happy Few? That's not easy to
explain,
because the Happy Few are indescribable.
Although few,
they come in all races sexes & nationalities
eras ages societies conditions
& religions.
They may be poor or rich
(though if they're born poor, they generally
remain so, and if born rich, soon grow poor)
young or old (though
they rarely live long enough to grow old)
ugly or beautiful (truth be told, even
when vulgarly denominated ugly,
in REALITY they're beautiful; but REALITY
is seldom seen by people . . .
Anyway. Objectively, in good faith
& fair dealing, we hereby
certify
that the H.F. are all and always

mo-st-beau-tiful,
though people can't see that for themselves).
And finally suffice it to add,
in this explicative presentation,
that in their great many variations
they may be flagrant & famous, or hidden
& unknown
(though when they're famous, Fame doesn't usually show
much eagerness to embrace them alive
but prefers to enjoy them in a posthumous clutch
once they are gone &
deceased).

          ?And where do they reside, as a rule? There is no rule.
Indeed their proper natural element
has never been discovered, so far, by biology.
You can find some in the himalayas & by the sea, in the
     city & in the desert, uptown or downtown,
in narrow alleys or on highways
maybe on abstruse planets or moons
or even inside ministries—remember Henri Beyle—
but never in the high echelons of bureaucracy
or in the various capacities of official authority
to which they have always shown a severe allergy.
You may meet them
at the university in the tavern in the factory in jail
     in brothels in convents at the theatre

                                        in the dance hall or cafe
among savants or illiterates in ghettoes in the Kasbah in
                         the subway on a jet plane
in the old people's home or the mad people's hospital.
They might crop up in the least suitable climates

and hide just where you least expect them.
In fact the H.F. are
fateful accidents of the Perpetual Motions
original seeds of the Cosmos, flying at the four winds'
                                    whim between fantastic poles
and flourishing in any soil.
Though most often they return
to certain (barbaric) orients & obscure (derelict) zones
where no one's in the vicious habit of murdering prophets
or slaughtering
poets.

? And what does U.M. mean? Obviously, this too is an
                                    abbreviation:
it stands for *Unhappy Many*.
? And who are the Unhappy Many?   Just ALL
the others.
? But what is the actual sign by which you can tell on
                                    sight
that degenerate minority from this normal majority?
    Clearly the real answer here
would be: HAPPINESS. But (c.f. above)
HAPPINESS
often seems invisible to Everyman
stye-eyed & infected as he is
with the too many smokes
of unreality. And so the saying goes:
'There's no such thing as happiness.'
UNREALITY is the opium of the people . . . And for a
general detox & rehab
the cure is an exercise of heroic difficulty . . .

!!No thanks, lady! none of that for us! nothing doing!!
!rather, will you please urgently produce
the name surname & address
of some certified authentic H.F. or other,
so we can have a little stock here
without all the fuss & bother!

    Ah—yes, ladies and gentlemen,
I understand! But, in all honesty,
all my good intentions notwithstanding,
I cannot fulfil Yr. esteemed order
I'm afraid: you see, I lack the standing,
the faculty & competence.
Have patience. And besides (if you'll excuse me) even
                    the best society
recommends names be handled with a certain—uh—
                    reticence.
It's a known fact
that, by their nature, H.F. types,
if not always kept under surveillance, are certainly
                    viewed with suspicion
by the Authorities. How do I know
Your suave debonair looks
might not hide some spying crooks
from the police station??
. . . No offence, ladies & gents—I take it back!
In fact, in goodwill & reparation
reconciling courtesy and prudence
I shall hereby, in Your esteemed presence,
start leafing through the UNIVERSAL ENCYCLOPAEDIA
and without further ado
abstract at random for You

the epigraph of some (defunct) H.F. of international fame
inscribed therein,
so as to enrich Your experience and further Your
culture.

Here we are—for the moment it might suffice
to record & indicize

e.g.

THE FOLLOWING:

BENEDICTUS Spinoza
(*the feast of the hidden treasure*)
Died banished
aged 45
in 1677

GIORDANO Bruno
(*the great Epiphany*)
Burnt alive
aged 52
in 1600

ANTONIO Gramsci
(*the hope for a real City*)
Died of prison-house
consumption
aged 45
in 1937

SIMONE Weil
(*the intelligence of saintliness*)
Died of voluntary starvation
in hospital
aged 34
in 1943

ARTHUR Rimbaud
(*the sacred adventure*)
Died of gangrene
in hospital
aged 37
in 1891

JOAN Tarc
known as of Arc
(*the invisible Thrones*)
Burnt alive
aged 19
in 1431

WOLFGANG
A. Mozart
(*the voice*)
Died of typhus
aged 34
in 1791
buried with a pauper's funeral

GIOVANNI Bellini
aka Giambellino
(*the wholesome eye lighting
the body*)
Died of common old age
in 1513

PLATO of Athens
(*the reading of symbols*)
Died of common old age
in 347 BC

REMBRANDT
Harmensz van Rijn
(*the light*)
Survived his loved ones
and died aged 63
in 1669

2

PARENTHESIS

TO THE H.F.

(How now O you dead you with the other
happy ones healed of all mourning
your present conversation means
that finally your contradictions don't exist
outside of our temporary gossip.
The unfathomable arabesque
is given for the joy of its movement, not for the solution
                                                          of its
theorem.
In the end your differences don't matter
because
every step of joy, that has joy as its departure and
                                        direction, is destined
always to the only place of rest
and freedom from all desires, first and foremost
from the absurd desire for a solution
to the theorem.
Your blessing is in knowing
that even the desire for paradise is servile.
The game is divine because there is no promise
or hope of any gain.

And right in this Impossible
is the luminous crux of the theorem, the centre of value
of every city: of the sidereal Jerusalem and
Marx's republic, of the Polyteia
or of Eden . . .
That point is the wholeness of the mind
—of course the busybody bosses fear that
as much as their own death. And there's the rub:
for fear is itself servile.
The game is divine because it meddles and capers with
                              the demented, scandalous bull
of death.
Your freedom is in knowing
that any goal of victory, all expectation of applause
is servile.
Your beauty is unashamed at being reviled or spat upon.
                              Other, other is its restraint.
And your unparalleled, ultimate grace
is that your beauty
DOES NOT CONCERN YOU.
O hoodlum more fabulous than the Aztec and Altaic fable
                              O lone migrant kid
with no court or family nothing but your shaman drum
                              and your voices
from the seventh constellation your nest to the ruinous
                              hamada of hell
searching for innocence your only lover your first wedding
                              feast

O heavenly drummer
you possessed sorceress of tortures

little peasant hand leading your dear tribe against the
                                                    leviathans
immaculate little sister
last cut down dove of the floods
beauty of the Song of Songs camouflaged behind those
                    funny, short-sighted schoolgirl glasses you wore
sacred tenderness
bitch of the streets slain by stoning
wrathful excommunicated heresy you the Credo In Unum
                                                    & Hallelujah
you the howled night of ghettoes & the starlit window
Etz Chayim
Jew & Marrano atheist subversive you Christian smile of
                                                    patience
your ultimate face in the silt-pale flab of consumption
grace disfigured by the stupors of jailhouse winters you
                                                    maturity
and childhood you the sedentary teacher and errant boy
                            you the dear cheek untouched
        by puberty on the shoulder of the moribund old man
you poor crisscross of wrinkles on the hand inventing the
                            dimples of the carnal infant
you the caress
    the pariahs beautiful as Madonnas under your caress the
                    eye of the born blind awestruck in Emmaus
through your caress
you
the motherly shroud texture of fresh love over the body
                                                    of leprosy you

the enchanted weft of breath inside the grave cloth of
                                                                Lazarus
you the tragic attention
fugue of your lullaby through the nine choirs of silence
O lacrimosa
dies!
Yes
I know
the wondrous game
turns to nausea when the angelic trumpeter swells his
                        cheeks already beaded with death's sweat
into a puny mimed blowing straining towards deaf mute
      vanities, an inaudible agonal bubble
                        stranded this side of the great migrating
vibrations of the *Tuba Mirum.*
I know
adolescence likes to rush right to the top of every stairway,
                        never mind if it's Jacob's ladder
and having to drag yourself around
struggling on crutches
is heart-breaking and idiotic—let alone
making you look like some comic strip clown.
NE VOUS LAISSEZ JAMAIS AMPUTER.
I know
that for a girl starting out on the ordeal of the Cross
and arriving alone at the delirious guilt of exile
the foreign hospital bed is a harrowing maze of barbed
                                                                wire
where her Jewish little body yields itself up
to suicidal fever

so as to consume inside itself the slaughter of all death
                                                    camps.
I know
the incarnation of the son of man, burning alive at the
                                        stake, will not rise
whole and unscathed like the species of bread and wine
offered up at Sunday fairs
but writhe like a puppet
in the Sabbath pictures of hell,
reduced to a grume of nerves. I know
that no rape against nature is as much of an aberration
from nature
as the law of the jailhouse. I know
that the pitiful infirmities of the body will not edify
the mind (that's just blah blah) but rather
corrupt and degrade it. And that of all possible evils
come to ravage this
vulnerable marked substance
none is more humiliating
than common old age. I know
I
KNOW.
Yet for you
my voicing pity is now one
with your ancient weeping: one same risible object
of compassion.
Your substance is in knowing
that this lacerating machine we call *the body*
was but a sepulchral refuge
of fear and of desire.

The eye is invented when the view wants a limit
the ear, when sound needs a wall.
Farewell,
O dead, you splendour music of the theorem.
May you all forgive, may you, One, forgive
us if we cannot die, and so we don't know
about dying.
We are the hunger to exist
the parasite swarm of a tomb seen in a dream's delirium.
Buzzing with death's decay this cloud is deaf
to the concentric circles melodiously rustling
towards the liberating unintelligible mantra
your and our only name.
Given to the absurd multiplication of the spectrum
the faceted eye of delirium
cannot see
the child body
our your body
unique
present
actual
alive
O you real, haggard
happiness.)

3

TO THE U.M.

Happy New Year. Here we go again. It's January the first.
AD 1967.
Twentieth Century. Atomic era.
By the looks of it, year in year out
the Happy Few grow fewer & fewer
less & less happy.
Little wonder:
the Unhappy Many are too too busy
fabricating traffic-trading instituting organizing
    classifyzing propagandyzing
their huge indispensable happiness
to trouble themselves with the Happy Few's superfluous
minority
unhappiness.
One can notice nonetheless
the usual disquieting age-old phenomenon:
in actual fact, goodness knows why,
the unhappiness of the Happy Few is
way happier than the happiness
of the Unhappy Many!
The happiness of the Unhappy Many

is not allegro! is never allegro!
The Unhappy Many have to put up & shut up:
no matter how they fuss,
take it from us: THEIR HAPPINESS IS TETERRIMOUS!
and the unhappiness of the Happy Few
is allegro! A L L E G R O !
Anywhere, anyway, it's allegro: in the Arctic or the Congos,
    or be it among Cannibals & Ogresses
it's allegro!
How to explain it? Bah! Life's a riddle! nothing doing!
The Unhappy Many can damn their souls
struggling with renewed purpose one & all
against this paradoxical vexation
deploying all of their moral
industrial nuclear etc. energy
into some superoriginal creation
of unhappiness
against the Happy Few!
No way! No way! They can't do it! They've got to reckon up,
& swallow the same old bitter cup:
the unhappiness
of the Happy Few
is
allegro! ALLEGRO!
AL-LEG-RO!
In ghettoes
in harlems
in Siberia
in Texas

in Buchenwald
in jail
on the scaffold the electric chair
in suicide.
Absolutely irredeemably
irretrievably
ALLEGRO!
Its howls are allegro
its delirium is allegro
its blood is allegro
its stinks smell of furze & fresh jasmine
while the perfumes of the Unhappy Many smell like mould
                                     & dried urine.
We repeat: Unhappy Many, call it a day.
Live with it
O Unhappy Many, it's no use trying anyway.
There's nothing doing
noth-ing do-ing!
Your happiness is so sad you choke & wheeze
but the unhappiness
of the Happy Few
hooray
how free, how allegro it breathes!
How come this failed old farce must be repeated
after hundreds of thousand millions of disasters?
Yo, Unhappy Many! You should know the score by now: just
    back down, that's all you can do!
No matter how you pig-head around the place
nagging & rowelling ordering & sentencing & killing by
                                          ruling,
the final result is the same. Nothing doing!

NOTH-ING DO-ING!
Your happiness is sad and the unhappiness
of the Happy Few
is allegro
unrulyly absurdlyly loonyly
A L L E G R O !
Can you deny it?
That plank of old scrap wood
on which by the sacramental virtue
of the (authoritative U.M.) Pharisee
a blasphemous young Galilean
(supreme H.P.)
consumed his scaffold death
in the April of AD Thirty-three
was dewed with such bloodied freshness
that it buds anew every summer
in an eternal fantastic revolution! for one thousand
                                    nine hundred & thirty-four
years
olé! it grows allegro
as a sunflower
allegro allegro olé! like a sunflower tree
allegro allegro allegro like a forest of sunflowers
olé! olé!
whereas no object of sadness no matter how sad
—and make it real sad: not even an anonymous stretcher
                                    moored at the Morgue
nor a standard-issue bier tipped into the paupers' grave
nor a hospital counter sluice-rinsed after an autopsy
no no no

no object no matter how sad or most saddest ever feels or
                                                          looks
just as sad
as wretchedly dismally miserably
SAD
as the Supersuspensionspecialissuelatestmodelstretchlimo
bearing—in high uniform or reverend robe in stylish
double-breast or bishoply vestment in bat-sleeve Teutonic
                                        eagle or Russian cassock
in Chinese trouser suit or US-style slick guy jacket
& various other attires
always the same
& selfsame
always with hooked fingers & policing eyeball
the usual manias & phobias & musty old theories
the usual senile envy
& the same old might-is-right mug—
the Pharisee, who at the age
of 99999
still can't get round
to dying.
Oi! Yous! U.M.! still not cottoning on?
still in denial? The unruly yellow blouse
of Poet Volodya Mayakovsky (H.F. even in spite of himself)
murdered by one Filistenka Saddoff (U.M. of the Central
    Rappist Committee)
in the April of year 1930,
is here, is there, hooray! fluttering away
allegro allegro allegro like a yellow sail racing on the
                                        breezy morning sea

like a little flag on the finish line like a flyaway kite riding
high
like a star in the company of stars in the star-studded sky
like a newborn marigold flower
—while the regular good bourgeois shirt washed & ironed
& well-sanitized belonging to the above-mentioned
Filistenka Saddoff
(still settled on his little camouflage throne
—with his brain always stuck on belabouring
new reports & orders & sentences deportations persecutions
eliminations
of H.F.)
mamma mia how
sad that the regular good shirt is it's sad SAD
sad
sad like a worn-out butcher's apron hanging tattered &
spattered on a hook
no—make it sadder, sadder, much sadder!
sad
like a stale bandage used to wipe a urinal and then thrown
in the garbage
sad sad sad
sad like an old news sheet
wrapped round a piece of meat
from a gelding mutton
that's gone & rotten.
    What do you think, O Many? And I could expatiate
for a hundred thousand more pages. But I'll spare you all
that

(lest I should get the spews)

and close with some more recent news.
And you'll have to excuse me, U.M. of the Universe
if, in ultimate homage to my Italian home,
I dedicate this verse
to the new History of Rome.

    The slain voice of young kid
Rossi Paolo, university student (a H.F. by fate)
who with his fresh unarmed body went out to face
the obscene adult monster born of the copulation

                      between *Fuehrer* & *Duce*
(ideal models of good U. M. family man)
and there fell dead
in the April of year 1966
—hey, you, Roman U.M.! Hear it now,
that tragic voice in its early song—bless it,
    how allegro it is!
Manly, daring, boyish allegro!
ALLEGRO
allegro allegro
like the theme of the crossing in the *Magic Flute*
allegro
like twenty kid mandolins under the windows
of a pretty young girl feigning sleep
allegro like the duo
of a woodland sparrow with his acquaintance, a newly

                      returned migrant,
first thing in the morning, at the bright daybreak of the
    ascending
equinox,

allegro allegro allegro! Right in your face, U.M.! seriously
freely
victoriously
allegro.
Whereas, mercy, how sad
SAD
sad alas sad
sad
like a pent-up spent-out whistle blown by a pensioned
                                    policeman in his privy
sad like an advert on the telly selling soaps & creams for
                                 the skin of your dreams
like the virtuous smug *alalà* of the Lady Wife of Consul
                             Smuggles, sporting her mink coat
as she deigned to greet
the Lady Wife of Head of Maniple Desimone
smarting in her hogget coat
at the parade of prolific fascist Matronas
(Anniversary of the 1938 March on Rome) . . .
But no, no, I know, try as I might I won't find
—how can I—
a fitting comparison to well signify
how sad
how sad alas alas
SAD phonetically semantically morphologically sad
are the inured comical mature voices of present-day
                             PhDs (National Medal U.M.)
still busybodying with all the revered & belaureled &
                             betitled breath on them

to blow into the holes of the aforementioned (& as-yet bio-
     ethnologically unclassified)
crass sleazeball son of Benito & Adolf
so that he'll never deflate
but prosper & live between the walls
(excruciating in their fascist architecture)
where the Masterful Roman Authority
of the Academic Senate & Worshipful Rectorate
sits in state.
     Ah, Doctors, Doctors! at your age!
Why oh why,
WHY
Your Lordships, U.M. Doctors of the Universe
with all your phd-ing & stickleback-a-laureing
& professoring yourselves in Universities,
with all your history & geography, your wit-sharpening &
     machine-building & all your travels,
all the sciences you unravel
inventing atomic bombs & lunar flight
why won't you find a way to get it right,
this very basic lesson of experience?
I repeat, Your Lordships U.M., there is no way:
YOU DON'T STAND O N E CHANCE WITH THE H.F.
Those guys have known flight long before aviation
they've known the panacea long before
penicillin they know the resurrection
from the dead!
Don't kid yourself you can get rid of them.
You might well think you've gobbled them up—but then,

at the high point of your banquet
here they come again, jumping
right onto your plates.
They are unbelievable unconceivable inadmissible they're
all mad.
And don't lull yourself in the hope they can be
RESTANDARDIZED
& then paternally legitimized.
One poor Jew that never had anything to do with Your
Lordships U.M.
once said certain bastards are the salt
of the earth. How to remedy the blandness of our food
if Your Lordships do away with this salt's bite?
No salt, no life! This little teaching—you should get it right,
for what a huge mistake it'd be
(expecting as you do to lead our History)
to lack even the rudiments
of natural history!
Never mind. But apart from the scientific suicihomicidal
effect
to be imputed to your ignorance, what would in fact
be the specific ideal
of your paternal hope? TO ALL MARCH UNITED
UNDER ONE LOGO (U.A.)
TOWARDS THE ULTIMATE DAY
AND THERE CROAK BENIGHTED
ALL IN COMPACT ARRAY.
Brilliant deal!
So
this is the sensational slogan

of your forward thinking?! Does this look—to you—like
    the final goal
for the great worldwide collective?!
the superlative flower of the socially productive?
Your Lordships, there is
some mistake.

Luckily though
some trajectories are way outside your range.
In vain, O U.M. fathers, you take aim.
Since our chemistry won't stand the blanding of salt,
those H.F. kids just can't be caught.
Hooray!

Those guys won't let themselves be mummied & daddied
    like yours
who go to sleep like sweet little things
under the framed portraits of bosses
made in the image of Mother Queen & Father King.
They know of no mother or father.
Those born to bring allegro salt unto the earth
are worse than those who set off to take Jerusalem.
Mothers & fathers are forgotten.
But what's that to you? Since of course, for your own war
you can bank on the unhappy majorities
i.e. your legitimate posterities
that will stand obedient at the ready
because thanks to you
they're demented already.
And as for the other few,

you sit on your stocks of gas & rope, and wait & hope
for your next chance to silence (at least until their return)
those promoters of allegro commotion.
Meanwhile muddling any allegro temptation
in our poor minds with your saddest noises
so rebuilding your good times' foundations.
Convinced as per usual again
that the system will work, that this time you'll pull off the
scam

at long last your sad kingdom will have its day.
As it may.
But watch out
your lordships watch out
for surprises.

Know this, O mingy U.M. fathers of every land:
if the outraged body of the living still resists
in this your world of blood & teeth
it is because those unscathed voices still exist
coming through with their allegro news.
Against your squad groups & tortures & ordures
your careers enterprises expenses & flags & powder stores
your aims financial claims glories with no defeats &
fascist sashes & popish seats
against your wholesome ideology your nice police force
GPU Gestapo FBI MinCulPop OVRA RAPP & Co
and all your funeral litany
we only have that one timeless apotropy:
the allegro salt
of the Happy Few.

How are Your Royals & Presidents & Generals
Incomes & Monies? All well with Business?
All fine with The Family? How's the Lady keeping?
And how's the Bomb standing up to the test? Who's got the
best?
Capital Mama or Proletariat Dad?
Well done well done, congratulations. You're still regular sad.
Too alike. Too alike. Too sad and too alike
too alike and too sad. Too sad too sad
sad sad SAD. Don't you ever fancy being just a tad less sad?
Though of course if you like saddity, do by all means enjoy
your own.
This earth is not your property. We've been trying to
explain that to you
for centuries & millennia.
Our mamma didn't make us to serve your purposes.
She didn't give us eyes to look on your sad faces.
She didn't give us ears to hear your saddo blah blah.
Your war is not our war. We're on the allegro side,
we are for grace, that is
for happiness.
What's all your noise about anyway? Silence! Taisez-vous!
Shut up!
Make way! Out of the way!
That's quite enough!
We are
finally objectively & ultimately
bored with you.

And you, poor Many girls & lads,
unhappy stupid children

of unhappy stupid dads,
why let yourselves be maimed?
How long will you stay slaves? Don't you know that in the
long run
servitude is no longer a necessity
or a virtue or fatality
but a vice?
How long before you promote yourselves to coming of age?
Don't you ever fancy finding out
about your real unhappy condition?
or using a part of your spare time
for some real happy meditation?
You'll say: 'We prefer TV with its fortybillion licencees.
These vaunted H.F. you wave at us
—there's just a handful of them, really. Strength in numbers.'
'Well—I would say—that depends. I mean, for instance,
who is better: a handful with their balls about them, or
fortybillion castrated? Who knows?'
'Give over, old missus,
you're stressing us out with your abstract talk. Just the facts
now.'
'You're right, children.
OK, here are the facts: those numbers the U.M. have, where
do they get them?
Those numbers,
that's you: sad (or maybe not so sad) but true.
But don't you ever—ever!—fancy meddling with the figures
of the ordinary sum?
gleefully overturning the humdrum
millennial history? finally & forever kicking down the doors
of the magic chamber

where for hundreds & thousands of years those sad fathers
of sadness
have sat locked in their wheeling & dealing?
Air, air
for this infected prison. We are travelling in the police van
of ignorance.
We don't know the beginning or the end. With every
instant we hurtle towards the
unknown destination.
We'd better take any chance run to any hope follow any clue.
Who knows what's in store at the next station?
Heed my poor song.
It might not be long
perhaps even before Judgement Day
before you're outnumbered by that mad H.F. band.
You might want to start some kind of training
to prepare for that happenstance.
It would be a magnificent extravagance
if all together we took a leap over the bad times
in a HAPPY ALL allegro finale! That'd be best.
Perhaps, the first essential secret
of happiness can still be found.
What matters is—once again—to set off on the quest.

There's this guy
(anonymous H.F.) who
was thrown to the lions under the Caesars as a slave
thrown to the lions again under the Flavii as a Christian
throat-slit in Technotitlan as a female virgin

burnt alive by the Popes as an unholy heretic
burnt alive again by the Bishops of Flanders as an obsessed
sorceress
executed by the Tsars as a revolutionary
hanged by Stalin as an anarchist
raided by fascists as a male of military service age
gassed in Buchenwald as a Jew
lynched in Dallas as a nigger
eaten by Zulu cannibals as a whitey
drowned in a flood in Friuli as a Friulian
bombed in Vietnam as a mother in childbed
crushed under crumbling buildings in 1900 Agrigento as
a seller of lupin beans on a street corner;
currently living happily incognito in a cave in some tibet,
now goes around saying that

the great revolutionary manifesto of the extremist H.F.
has been printed in myriads of copies by day & night
ever since before languages
& scriptures existed. But for all legible things
there always exists another, hidden reading,
& if the living lose the code books,
so does the author of the scriptures,
even though he's called God. In fact, the living are the house
    of this one God,
so if they close their windows, the dweller in the house
will go blind.
We must open again the lights of our eyes
for him to regain his sight.

Perhaps
in heaven doesn't mean a kingdom come, nor even
an other's region. Perhaps, the double
image *on earth as it is in heaven* can be read
as one image doubled in its own mirror.
Perhaps, *turn and become like children* teaches that the
    ultimate intelligence of the end
resides in identifying with the beginning. And the
                       mysterious trinity
is explained by the seed that, while begetting, begets itself
through the seamless blood of its own virgin death.
As for your *neighbour*
you (I'm speaking for you too, you half U.M. writing here)
can recognize him naturally in those who are born
nobody knows where from, & die to go nobody knows
                           where
with no one to save them from grief or spare them from
                           death:
no mothers or fathers on earth or in heaven.
Alone and homeless: no more, no less
than you.
And here the Anonymous cave writer is in fact sure
that in the difficult command: *Love him as thyself*
the *as* must be read as meaning *because.* BECAUSE
the *other*—the *others* (H.F. & U.M. & sapiens & faber & dog
            & toad & every other deathbound life)
ARE all yourself: not your fellows or peers or companions or
    brothers
but that same one

YOUR
SELF.

    Such things (as s/he would have it) are not new: in fact
        they've been clear since the beginning
for the wild, the banished, the lost they were addressed to.
The ambiguity of the letters is not casual,
rather it's an INTENTION proclaimed as a searing challenge
by the mystery that shouts: who wants to hear, let him hear!
But the total Revolution will only come
when that proper reading (*as = because*)
comes no less natural than your own breath,
or the discovery, in common infancy,
of 'I', the first person pronoun.
So will you immediately
have recognized yourself: & so will
thy promised
allegro *kingdom*
come to you . . .

    Question: But WHEN?
    Answer: There is no WHEN.
    Q: But WHERE?
    A: There is no WHERE.
    Q: But then, HOW?!
    A: Well, anyhow . . .
    Q: But in the end, will it be
        TRUE
        or not?
    A: And you are asking *me*,
        O my poor
        boy-girl?!

Once upon a time
there was a little orphan girl, a very very poor girl: she was
about a year old
when one fine day, having been given a brand new bonnet
(which instantly enamoured her, because it was deep blue)
she was led for the first time in front of a mirror.
And in this unknown place she immediately recognized
her cherished bonnet
on a perfect stranger's head. Jealousy was tearing her apart
and desperately she searched behind the mirror
hunting high & low for the bonnet thief.
In that instant a spell fell upon her and doomed her
so the bewitched little creature is still there,
behind the back of the dust-blackened mirror,
blindly investigating the hideous theft
with her pretty little blue bonnet
on her head.

    That's all. See you. Ciao.

II

The World Saved by Kids

An Epic in Various Songs
Joined by One Subversive Refrain
& Closed by an *Envoi*

*Soñaba yo que tenia
alegre mi corazón
mas a la fé, madre mia,
que los sueños sueños son.*

(Ancient folk song)

1

SONG OF THE SCAFFOLD

When I was older
I used to work on a suburban building site down on the plain,
though we lived outside town, halfway up the ridge.
My name was Simone, nickname Simó,
I was a building foreman,
and as a helper and hoddie
I was dragging along my youngest son Rufus, who was
                                    going on sixteen,
and nicknamed Longface,
because he always kept to himself, always sulking.
Early one morning, coming down from our neighbourhood
                                    with him,
—without a word passing between us, as usual—
going down the rough slope towards the site,
we came across a military squad
taking one to torture. But this man,
skinny and beaten to a pulp,
didn't have it to climb up the slope, loaded as he was with
                                    his own scaffold
—because he had to carry it himself, that was the law—,

and his legs were giving every two steps,
until he fell sideways on the slope. So the squad sarge
roughed him back up to his feet and shouted an order to me:
"Ere, you—you look hardy enough! Come give a hand
to the king of the Jews.'

               There was no arguing with that,
so I rushed over
to obey. Close up, the man
looked nothing at all like a king,
or even a dangerous criminal,
but the lowest of the low unfortunates.
His face, a mask of blood.
His body, battered and shuddering, down to the ribs and
                         nearly broken in two,
half naked in its few filthy rags.
His feet, bare and small, black with sweat and dust.
And, aside from those uniforms in the squad,
no one else was around, either near him or at some distance,
to walk with him as he went to his doom.
No mother or brothers or friends,
no doctor, not even a priest. The only follower,
late coming, was Longface,
waiting a little way off, ready to walk behind us,
the greasy paper bag with our dinner in one hand
(that day, I remember, it was fish in sauce)
and his face longer than ever. All this I barely had time to
                         notice,
because, as soon as I heaved the scaffold onto my
                         shoulders,

my eyes went dim—I was near blinded
with the massive strain. It felt like that wooden beam
had another one inside made of lead, so heavy it was,
and I wondered how that breathless lazarus
could have dragged it even for a short stretch. Me, I'm no
athlete,
but I'm strong enough, and well used to loads; still
I was hard put to move my feet, dripping sweat, panting and
wheezing with the struggle. But suddenly, right then,
a weedy voice cries out 'STOP! Everyone stop!!!' And there
goes Longface,
planting himself squarely in front of the squad,
his face so black with anger
that everyone did stop dead. And he goes (in that broken
teenage voice of his
that's like a little off-key trumpet): 'You shits, you bunch
of stinkers,
armed forces of my bollocks,
first of all, if you're sending someone back to his Maker,
at least send him back with the face he'd given him
when he sent him down 'ere.
And second, you swine, you bloody trollops,
I don't know how you stop your bellies bursting
with all the shit you've got inside you. With one—one!
load to carry
between the seven or eight of you (*armed forces*, you call
yourselves!)
you just can't hack it, and dump the lot
on an old man and a bag o' bones! 'Ere, give it 'ere,

I'll get that twig! And you' (to the sarge,
scrunching the paper bag with the fish dinner into his hand)
'here—carry this for me at least, will ya!' I was standing
                                                        there,
my eyes popping, my head spinning,
thinking I'd ended up in the loony bin.
And in a strangled voice I was cursing Longface, saying
                                        you prick, you shithead,
and, what the fuck's up with you?! you want to ruin us?!?
    But the militiamen, they
were standing stock still, and straightaway
followed my boy's order with no argument,
whether they were unprepared for such phenomenon,
or with their special (retarded) mentality
had presumed he was some generalissimo in plain clothes
or some high representative of the Diplomatic Corps!
Anyway. No matter how desperately I protested, expecting
                                        my poor Longface
to croak right in front of me under that impossible load,
the scaffold was set on Rufus' skinny little shoulders!
But as soon as it landed on him, I saw him grow pale,
unable to get back on his feet, and start raging
till his face was drenched in tears.
The whole squad was standing there at attention
as if they'd seen nothing special,
but the blood mask, he started laughing
quietly to himself.
And instantly

you can see Longface smiling with his eyes,
and then, scrawny as he is (he never was a muscle man)
and dwarfed by that pole as tall as three of him
stand up free and easy
like he was carrying the tiniest little hodful of bricks
and start up, faster and faster and fresher with every step
so that at the end he looked like a sparrow
with that forked old trunk for wings.
And at the same time
the squad men had resumed their march, in military step,
without noticing anything new,
as if they'd been turned there and then into puppets
with two bolts for eyes, sheet-iron ears
and perfect clockwork innards
responding to the Boss' orders.
And so the cortège climbs up the slope.
Strutting ahead was the sarge
the paper bag with our dinner in his right hand,
holding it carefully a little way from his breastplate
like it was a chamber pot.
Behind him, between the double martial escort,
on one side, myself, load-free and stockfish-stunned;
on the other, Longface, carefree under the scaffold;
and between us two the blood mask
who just kept laughing
to himself. But at the last bend
in view of the levelled mountain top
that's like a chewed-up bald head,
the laughter broke in his throat as he looked up

and he started shaking.
At the same time
we saw that clot of blood on his face
dissolving into a vapour. And he was coming out of it,
                                        shaking,
his face washed and untouched, in healthy high colour
under his black curls drenched in salt water
like a hale young sailor fresh out of the sea.
Perhaps he hadn't even noticed
this change he'd just gone through. He was laughing a little
like before again, in the same natural way,
standing next to us,
so near I felt his breath tickling my skin.
He spoke in a singing basso voice
I'll not ever forget.
And said: 'Simó and Longface, my good friends!
we must say goodbye now. I won't keep it from you:
this is a morning of fear and agony for me.
But never mind. Let it pass,
and don't sorrow for me.
I know one thing
and now want to secretly share it with you
even though I know it's not enough for us. But pity the
                                        poor others here who do not know!
For myself I am certain of it, because by now I can see it
(though even seeing it is not enough for us!)
and you mustn't doubt it. Believe in me as a witness.
I say unto you:

EVEN IF IT SETS US SHAKING
IN FEAR AND AGONY,
ALL OF THIS,
IN TRUTH AND SUBSTANCE,
IS NOTHING
BUT A GAME.'

2

SONG OF JUDAS AND OF THE WEDDING

Including

The Clandestine Song *of the Great Masterwork*

With the Chronicle of the Little Fool

Or *Pazzariello*

When I was a lad
I was called Rufus—well all right, Longface,
as you'll have gathered from the previous song.
And here I go now, singing of what happened next.
The sun was scorching hot—it must have been about half
past eight

when my father and I
left that guy on the mountain with the militia, who'd
briskly set to work

raising the scaffold,
and started back on our own down the slope
taking shortcuts
to make our way quickly to the building site.
My father had under his arm the paper bag with our dinner
he'd got back from the sarge,
and I was walking any which way, head down, without
looking back,

to avoid seeing the top.

But halfway down,
just as the city comes into view,
from up above we heard a frightening scream,
like of a beast dragged to the slaughterhouse
and powerlessly rebelling in its last resistance.
And right then, tearing away from my father,
I threw myself into a headlong run,
at random down the slope, alone, like in some catastrophe.
At that moment
the only thing I wanted was to destroy the world,
and with rage roiling inside me as I ran, I felt easily capable
                                            of it,
so much so that I was already thinking: 'Where do I start?'
while in the meantime
that one short scream I'd heard, rebounding through the caves,
was prolonged into a chaos of voices, so as to sound like many
    people screaming
closer then further away, towards the place of a universal riot;
and I too felt like I was running to that place. Until I found
                                     myself
alone in the middle of the dry riverbed,
in the deserted lower zone of the mountain
this side of the underwood, where the echoes had faded away.
  Then finally I knew it was all over.
And slowing my step
I felt emptied in my mind, like I was floating at sea.
When from the distance I heard a great sigh,
and a singing basso voice reaching out to me,
like one making himself known by leaning towards me
                                    from a boat,

said restfully:

'All is consummated.'
Now fading a little, now growing close, as if from a boat
                                        moved by the tides
joyfully it repeated: It is consummated. It is
consummated.
And finished with a soft laugh that ran through the air
                                        ahead of me
like a sail, or a young cliff gull
tempting me to the chase.
But as we entered the underwood
it faded away.

    I took a few more steps into the underwood,
doubtful as to whether I should take this route
to the plains road,
towards the building site.
And as I made my
uncertain way across a clearing,
right there, a little off the way but fully exposed to the light,
I saw a man, big, dark and bearded,
hanging by his neck from a branch, bending it with his
                                        weight,
so that his feet almost touched the ground.
He was fully clothed, with shoes on his feet,
his face already black and deformed,
slit eyelids showing a streak
of filmy eyes, a sort of sky-blue colour.
Clearly he hadn't been sentenced by law & order:
no sign on him of any beatings,
nor did he look malnourished, though scruffy and soiled.

On the ground, half hidden under his shoes,
was a scrap of paper that might have slipped from his fist.
And scrawled on it
in a peasant's crooked hand:
Cursed be the day I was born
and cursed the mother bore me.
  After reading it, I threw it back at him,
and turned to go there & then: by now,
there was nothing doing for him anyway.
But then I thought better
of leaving him exposed like some poor carrion;
even if he'd written *cursed the mother*,
he was his mother's son still, wasn't he!
so I scrabbled about to bury him as best I could,
right there, under the tree where he was hanging,
digging a rough ditch with my little flick knife,
and with a bit of tree trunk, and with my hands.
And as I moved around the tree in these preparations
I discovered
that thrown and torn and stamped into the ground
in the scrub and goats' droppings
were I don't know how many authentic thousand and ten-
                                        thousand notes,
adding up to the value of *many* a thousand liras!
It didn't seem right to leave them there to rot,
when I could spend them wonderfully well.
But no sooner had I touched them
that like some witches' treasure
they turned my fingertips to ice with such disgust
that in the end I settled for one one-thousand note
fallen a little way off and swaying like a cyclamen,

nice and ironed and almost brand new, with the photo of the
                              Homeland crowned as a queen,
and of our Emperor in plain clothes.
'These' I thought 'will come in well handy,
especially as Sunday's coming,
and knowing already that this week, as per usual, my pay
will end up full in my father's pocket,
and I'll be lucky if he slings me a bit of change
for half a packet of fags and maybe a coke . . .
but WITH THESE
at least I can buy a ticket for the match
—too bad I don't have a girlfriend!
I could take her to the cinema, and
then out for a pizza as well!'
And so I pocketed that thousand right away, leaving behind
     all the rest,
which I partly kicked under the soil I'd dug up,
without giving it a thought. In fact I was enjoying
turning all that money to garbage—the fuck-may-care
                         whim of some great lord. And good day to you.
    It took me over half an hour
to dig a hole the size of that dead man,
who was of more than average height,
and wide in the shoulders and chest. And when, holding
                              him up as best I could,
I sliced with my knife through the noose tied around him,
it felt as if he'd thrown himself into my arms at once
with the weight of a colossus, nearly toppling me backwards.
I was shaking, drenched in sweat,
after offloading him into the ditch. But without stopping for
                                        breath,

in the rush to get him out of my sight,
I covered him up straightaway, kicking the mound of soil

back in,

until the hole was filled. Then, knock-kneed
and breathless with exhaustion, I squatted on the top
for a moment's rest,
and started patting the ground to make it level.
Lying under there, now, that dead man made me feel sorry.
It seemed as though his frightened mind
couldn't understand his own end, as though he was crying out:
'Help! Oh I'm in trouble! Where am I?!'
thrown back into that hole, his ugly frizzy head tossed on
    one side,
how he had ended,
face-up in that graceless pose—how he had ended.
Already in my memory he seemed not quite so ugly
as I'd seen him a little earlier.
And I couldn't leave him like that, without a greeting.
Before walking away,
with my heart pounding, I put my breath to the ground
as if to whisper into his ear, like a sworn secret,
something forbidden.
And I said to him: 'Listen, my friend.
YOU MUST NOT be scared:
I know a secret I've learnt from a trusted friend
and you must understand it is true, though it might not

seem so.

Listen to me:

> ALL OF THIS
> IN TRUTH AND SUBSTANCE

IS NOTHING
BUT A GAME.'

My ears were buzzing
and I thought I saw shadows of flies in the air all around.
I decided I wouldn't go to the building site that day,
and no longer cared about my father or anything else.
I didn't care for anything
except lying down on the ground, right there or anywhere,
and going to sleep.
And I did fall asleep straightaway. And, lying next to mine,
I could feel another body reaching close.
I didn't turn round, for fear it might be the dead man,
but a voice like a young girl's
started laughing and whispering in my ear:
Longface! Longface!
and then I did turn around.
It wasn't the dead man, it was a little bride
alive and kicking!
breathing and sleeping next to me.
She wore an embroidered smock
and nothing else. She had clean and rounded flesh,
a pretty face.
I thought: 'Look high and low through the big wide world
you won't find one fairer, guaranteed!
This is a little queen of primary beauty!
And yet, she is mine!'
    Right then she opened her eyes
that looked like two little gold leaves inside a pretty little
                                                    bunch of roses,

and first of all she says to me: 'Do you love me? and will you
always love me?'
I got muddled, went all red, and replied: 'Eh? . . . er . . . '
She on the other hand is serious & self-assured, and resolutely
says: 'I love you!
I love you more than my own eyes, I love you more than my
own life,
more than the light of day! more than the stars!
And I will love you always!
For all the time of my life,
and beyond life!'
'Crikey!' I admired her, and said to myself, 'What lovely
thoughts! really of special
authentic loveliness! Better than a poem,
the way she speaks!
What am I going to tell her now? she's lucky to be able to
talk like that! but I
can never find a thing to say! Even if I start thinking, I'll think
about it all right,
but won't find a thing. Except when I get angry,
then words come much easier. But who's ever going to
get angry with this one?!' Meanwhile she was gazing at me,
full of happiness and ecstatic respect
like she was looking at James Bond,
with those two little hazel brown eyes sparkling gold
and giving me a fantastic sweetness. And she goes: 'Are you
happy?'
'Eh? . . . ' I said 'What a question!' '*What a question*,' she
noted grumpily,
'hardly means *Yes*!' 'Well . . . actually . . . ' I wanted to explain
myself,

but she'd gone all ornery on me: '*Yes* or *No*?' she insisted.
    And, afraid I'd offended her,
I shouted at the top of my lungs: 'YES!' 'Seriously? This *Yes*
                                                    you're saying,
    is it a real *Yes*?' 'Look!! You're getting right ornery now—
                            come on!' 'So give me the answer then!
Is it a real yes? is it?' 'Yesssssssssssss!' 'But if it is true, then
    why
did your eyes
flicker
with a dark
shadow?'
  And with that, she left me real speechless. Was she some
    fortune-teller?
Because truly
that happiness I was feeling
was such a real and endless splendour
that all the yeses said unto the ages of ages in every land
could have testified to it there and then
in a worldwide chorus.
But the thing with happiness
—the happier it is
the more it tears your heart, sort of.
In fact mine was bringing me
numerous worries, like flashing knives
threatening at the crossroads of many alleys in the dark.
First worry: surprise (she came
unexpected, and unexpected she might leave).
  Second worry: logic (logically, it would be too much luck,
if such a pretty bride staid married all her life
to a guy who—notoriously—is hardly a hunk . . .

Even my mother, who is my mother,
one day, years ago, when, just to be sure, I asked her opinion
—was I really bog-ugly or passable at least—,
could give me no better reply than:
'Eh, child! You're asking me? When even the proverb says
any old cockroach looks lovely to his mum')!!!
    Third worry: property (because this wife of mine,
as she is mine, must be only mine! But just as I see her so
                                                    pretty,
so might some wise-guys walking down the street—the
                            stinkers! the sonsofbitches!
the bastards! damn their sodding souls to hell!
But I'm going to break their faces all right—and their hearts
    too! If they so much as try, they're going to
            be sorry, them and their whole stinking lot!
                        Nah, they won't dare! No way!
    . . . First thing to do urgently, go straight to the Athletic
                                                    Stadium
for some practical judo classes . . .)
Anyway, she had guessed it: in my happiness
I would have been happy, but for the worries.
And she seemed to be reading my thoughts. Though I
    remained silent,
she looked at me with a sigh,
laid her little hand that looked like a carnation
on my dirty old paw
and said to me: 'What's worrying your soul?'
Today's no day for worries.
It is our wedding feast! Today we sing and dance
and stroll about
and have a good time.

And even if we're skint little gypsies, we'll
get by.
I know a one-eyed baker
and a deaf poultry-man and a lame greengroceress.
We'll steal their bread and their new zucchini and their eggs,
and I'll make you a nice pan haggity.
And I know a coffee-shop man who every regular afternoon
falls asleep sitting at the counter with flies buzzing all
                                                    round him.
And while he sleeps we can sit at the cafe
without paying a penny,
and watch the match on the telly.
'But there's no match today!'
I reminded her: 'there's nothing important going on till
                                                    Sunday,
when the squad are playing
Argentina.'
'Well then!' she replies, ' isn't that right? Perhaps you've
                                                    forgotten
it *is* Sunday today?' And she pointed upwards to a calendar
bearing the date:

> SUNDAY
>
> 30 APRIL.

??????? I was gobsmacked.
I knew for a fact it was Friday morning
when I fell asleep in this wood. Now this is Sunday morning:
so . . . did I sleep for two days then?
And there
a new worry jumped at me, with a threatening flash:
just like I didn't know I was sleeping for two days,
perhaps I'm still asleep

without knowing . . . ?

But she, fortune-telling as usual, looked at me again
with her giggly eyes:

'Whassamatter?'

she said,

'why are you clutching me that tight to your chest? why
are you staring at me with such despair?
would you like me any less, if I was a dream?!
But rest assured, I'm not a dream. In fact, as long as you were
 asleep, you couldn't see me,
but you can now that you're awake,
just like, if I was a dream, you couldn't see me now
but you could when you're asleep.'

And laughing she gave me a little love kiss. Then, very happily,
looking up towards a clock that was hanging in the leaves,
she exclaimed: 'Ten past ten!
we're just in time to turn the radio on! in five minutes
they're playing the programme of musical songs!!!!'

'What radio!'—I mumbled sarkily—some goat-head radio I
expect!

Can't you see we're in the middle of a wood?' But she, having
looked all around

as if she was scared of spies,
whispered warily: 'The CLANDESTINE RADIO!
I've got the set hidden here!' And fumbling along the hem of
her smock,

she took out from a seam
a sort of golden top, about the size
of a walnut.

'That thing?! does that even work?!' 'Of course it does!
Why wouldn't it?!'

'And how do you charge it?' 'Like this.' And placing the top
    on the ground, she gave it a push with her finger.
And the little contraption
beginning to spin, immediately
started beaming the signals
of radio waves.

                    From the distance approaching
were the instrumental notes of the famous song
Cielito Lindo
(the one that starts with *De la Sier-ra Mo-rena*
etc.).
Until they were interrupted by the voice of the speaker
who said 'This is CLANDESTINE RADIO!
The time is ten, fourteen minutes, and twenty seconds!
ATTENTION PLEASE! ATTENTION PLEASE! In half a minute
the vocal music programme will begin!
In ten seconds!! ATTENTION PLEASE!
... Five ... four ... three ... two ...
ONE!
And punctually
a hard and melodious voice
neither a man's nor a woman's
but sounding like a multiple instrument that can hit all the
    highs and lows it wants
and any varying expressions according to circumstance,
began to sing:

The caravan of the Great Masterwork is coming to town
fresh from Chicago and calling at Shanghai
on its way to Samarkand.
It has no horses or drivers or stokers or staff.
Leaving Shanghai it will call at Samarkand
on its way to Chicago.

Its double mobile revolving wings
are variously painted in many colours
on both sides.
Seen from too far away, those pictures are only blurred shadows,
and seen too close up, they're meaningless spots.

To enjoy the effect of true likeness
one must view them from a normal distance.
And therefore the caravan will stop
right in the middle of Empire Square,
which by way of its geometry
is well suited to the theatrical norm of vision
and will afford
indifferently from any point
of its entire surface
true enjoyment
of the said due likeness.

The effect also depends
on how the mobile wings
revolve

shift and

combine—

and it continually varies

according to the watchers' position,

be they still

or moving.

Those viewing the Masterwork from one side get frightened, scream and sob,

while those viewing it from the other are delighted, laugh or yawn.

And the parts are relentlessly inverted

with no rhythm, or continuity, or explanation.

No show is ever repeated.

From the moment the stage machinery is set in motion,

its movements are impossible to regulate.

The sequence of the scenes is unpredictable.

Choosing a place in advance, even if one could,
would offer no reliable guarantee.
And the trick of moving about during the show
offers nothing but some crazy gamble
where the odds are a thousand to nought.
All told, in the end,
as regards the compared effects of theatrical vision,
all viewing points are alike.
Even from the official box
—apart from the advantage of being able to sit down—
one can see nothing but the usual obsessive quintain.

When the Great Masterwork is announced in town
contrasting rumours spread far & wide.

The notices posted on each & every street
offer no explanation.
The title of the forthcoming show
is only given by a number
endlessly printed in tiny characters so as to cover the whole poster
and complicated by additions, subtractions & multiplications,
and signs & letters of al-jabr wa l-muqabala.
Try as you might to work out the total,
the figure resulting is always another.

And this leads to quarrels, accusations & trials.
Invisible recorders & camouflaged informers
are put to work.
All around the streets they come
strutting back:

the Patriots, the Plague Orders Undertakers, the Decorations, the Shareholders, the Pimps, the Most Moral
Fathers,
the Arcadias, the Hangmen, the Immaculate Ladies, the Laureates, the Loins, the
Hooked Pin, the Omicron Weapon,
in short several hundred ugly mugs, ugly bags, ugly squirts & most ugly sorts
with over seven thousand five hundred
plain clothes police.

The city swells & deforms, the crass pig-out cars multiply
sleazily, they rape her, breaking crazily
into her tender tricuspids, mitrals & semilunars!
and they laugh
biting & scratching in a chorus of unspeakable junk iron
and blasting out of their cavernous behinds
a vile cancerous cloud mass.

On every wall one can read:
LONG LIVE THE GREAT MASTERWORK!
Optimism reigns everywhere. Pessimism
is not of the people.
In every neighbourhood queues are formed
in front of the betting shops.
But the news circulating about the programme
is all arbitrary
and unreliable.

When at last the caravan of the Great Masterwork arrives
and sets up camp on the square,
all rush over, dragging their old people, kids, babies
& transistor radios (since the show is mute).
Latecomers trample the others

and leap over the queues. Rows and fisticuffs
break out. The throng thickens in the chaos.
The little ones start wailing. Families call out desperately to one another.
The guards' whistling increases. Water cannons are brought out. All present,
dripping and bitter, take it out on the harmless minorities.
There's bad news of people collapsing & dying in the stampede
but all the time the corpses ranked in the throng
pop back up on their feet, like sad bogeymen standing in tangled straw.
Hospital sirens wail, morgue & police
vans race around.
Laughing & tear gases are brought out.
Everyone is writhing among laughter & crying, a fraternity of spasms. Finally
one can see a little movement

in the VIP box

and all start clapping in unison
in a universal crescendo of applause.

They're here! The Ambassadors! the Generals!
The Academy of Culture & Discipline!
The Clergy!
The Noblewomen!
The School! The Charity! The Godliness of the Family! The Trades!
The Television!
The Noble Guards of the Superatomic Arm!
The Financial Police!
The Race!
The State Monopolies!
The Repression of Crime & Murder!
The High Commissions! The Prefectures! The Presidency!!

He's here,

the Emperor!!!!

But a huge thundering of cog wheels calls all eyes

towards the contraption of the Great Masterwork:

the extravagant and solitary machine

has set itself in motion!

The show unfolds among deafening comments

that turn into arguments, clashes & battles.

While for anyone who should try to storm the caravan

or smash the mechanisms to see how they might work

or rebel against the local supervisors

or act delirious or agitated

there are scaffolds and various instruments of torture

promptly rigged up on the corners of the square

with manacles & chains, trepanning lamps & straitjackets,
hunger cages, caustic baths, cutter hoods & centrifugal cots
and every other sort of similar edifying or purging contraption;
while the leash comes off on the werewolves, the blood-drinking rams
and the castrating scorpions, eaters of tongues & hands.

And so, triumphant over the barbarians and the unworthy,
the Great Masterwork rolls along on its way.
The census of the latest show
records all, absolutely all our townspeople
as present on the square.
In the deserted neighbourhoods both in the centre
and on the outskirts of town,
the only living beings left were the dogs,
who are not allowed anywhere near the Great Masterwork,

and so had set up a heart-breaking howling
from inside the barred-up & abandoned dwellings.

(Truth to tell, the cats were out there too,
capering up the switched-off traffic lights,
whiling the afternoon away on the empty stands
of traffic wardens, or
strolling around in numerous gangs
between the road markings—
in short, wholly giving themselves up
to their anachronistic cattings.
But then that lot
must be counted out of course
being antisocial barbaric untameable inferior
belonging as they do to a
Hamitic-Semitic race . . .)

. . . .

. . . By the way & wayside,

let it be recorded herein that before the New Social Reform

there still was at large in the city

a guy known as the Pazzariello.

Who, on account of his

scarce reasoning faculties

couldn't tell weekdays apart from Sundays

(thinking perhaps everyday was a Sunday!)

And so

while all the citizens were crowding

around the Great Masterwork,

he alone, as per his usual, was found wandering around

the streets, playing *Cielito Lindo*

on his ocarina,

with his hundred thousand little curls fluttering in the wind, his little scarf around his neck, his odd shoes,

and the happy childish face of a regular starveling.

(Only just bewildered to find himself

the only human walking among so many cats).

   At times, when he'd happened around the square,

seeing all that bedlam & rage,

he'd started laughing

thinking they were shooting some gangster movie.

Clearly, for him,

the arrival of the exceptional caravan

of the *Great Masterwork*

was the same as the passage of a standard lorry!

The sensational rumours anticipating the event

were, to his unkempt head, no more important

than rolling drums might be to a

fluttering little flag!

To him, the programme posters were as good as scrawls

seeing as he couldn't read,

let alone (!) count.

All he was able to do

was play *Cielito Lindo*

on his ocarina.

Ask him the most basic information

i.e. his

personal details,

and no matter how he broke his brain (so bad his forehead would be beaded in sweat!)

he would evince a fatal incapability not only of replying

but even of grasping the lit-er-al sense

of the request!!

'Your name and surname?' And he, dreamily: ' . . . ? . . . '

'Your place and date of birth?' And he: ' . . . I were born a Little

Foolish . . . '

And so on.

But who was he anyway?! how was he born?! Bah!

Some said they'd heard him declare in dead earnest

that he'd been born in the Great Flood

from the wedding of a she-ass

with a hailstone. According to more reliable sources

it seems they'd found him naked, a chit of three or four weeks, caked in the mire of his own piss

in the rubble & dust of the bombings of the Eighth World War

some eighteen years ago.

All right. But what class of rubble & dust?

Well-to-do, or raggedy-assed? Proper, or

sleazy? Of SUP.,

or inf. race? Bah!... After very careful investigations

carried out to no

avail,

the 'Pazzariello ID' case was filed

away.

We hereby produce for your information

the detailed record of the identification

of the subject in question,

as form-filled, stamped, registered, numbered & filed

c/o the Imperial Prefecture,

Secret Archives.

Attention please! Attention please:

SUBJECT   *the unknown known as Pazzariello.*

NAME AND SURNAME
RACE   *doubtful.*   *question mark.*
FATHER   *not known.*   NATIONALITY   *stateless.*
                                                 MOTHER   *not known.*
PLACE AND DATE OF BIRTH   *double question mark.*
SEX   *happy and magical.*   MARITAL STATUS   *kid.*
HEIGHT   *ft. five point seven.*
BUILD   *hale and hardy although underfed.*
HAIR   *darkish brown with longish curls hanging down.*
EYES   *brown speckled gold.*   MOUTH   *giggly.*   FACE   *pretty.*
DISTINGUISHING MARKS   *the curly hair of his underarms grows in the shape of stars.*
PROFESSION   *ocarina-playing vagrant.*

OTHER FEATURES:

EDUCATION *illiterate.*

I.Q. *zero.*   SPECIFIC SKILLS *inept.*

PUBLIC SERVICE OR PRIVATE EMPLOYMENT   *unfit.*   ARTS AND CRAFTS *incapable.*

SPORTS AND FITNESS *useless.*

ADDRESS *no fixed abode.*

MEANS OF SURVIVAL

zero.

!Attention please! Attention please! We have read out the identification record
of said Pazzariello, as registered filed etc.
as well as tampered with & interpolated & interpirated by an unidentified hand
in the Secret Archives etc. etc. etc.

!Attention please ! Attention please! The show continues
with the releasing
of some more useful information
on the above-mentioned individual:

   As concerns clothing, the same
used to kit himself out at the Dump for Unusable Refuse
seemingly finding said refuse
of much use.
E.g.:
one thigh boot plus one thick boot was a regular pair of shoes to him,
fitting readily & comfortably. In fact, he walked blithe & lithe in them
with the natural spring of his feet & legs
as if in two prancing little ballerina sandals!
And he roamed happily through the traffic jams eddying

around the city,

skipping between cars, dodging them by the millimetre, leaping over them

right on time

like a seven-month-old guanaco frolicking in his wood.

As concerns sustenance, at lunchtime

he'd turn up with a tin on the doorstep of second-rate inns

and blag a soup from various assorted leftovers, and then

he'd sit in a quiet corner on the pavement, usually in the company of one or more cats

with whom he'd share his soup, pouring an adequate ration out

directly on the flagstones.

At times, it happened that some cat, sniffing such pittance, would turn tail without even

tasting it.

And then he would shout: 'Sophisti-cat!'

and, downcast, set about

sharing it out fairly among the other cats, or sometimes

picked it up again & ate it himself.

    After lunch

he liked to go by a bar, where a barista boy he knew, an amateur music lover,

would give him a sip of alcohol left over from the cherries in brandy

to favour his inspiration.

And at night, he'd rig up some sleeping place: in winter, grottoes or doorways, and in summer, commons or

                                           boats

some nights alone, some others in the company

either of some filthy dog he didn't own, who in winter would warm him by panting and in summer cool

                                 him by waving its ears

or else of some unlicensed little uptown slut, who in summer would keep him cool

with her cool

little kisses

and in winter warm him up

with her hot
little kisses.
In such guise that bastard Pazzariello had sorted himself out with food shelter & clothing.
And so he could stroll around all day,
a happy,
merry
gypsy,
singing free of charge for one & all
his song *Cielito*
Lindo.

The public had tolerated him at first
as a funny, harmless little idiot.
But gradually, over some time,
accusations, remonstrations & complaints began to grow.

!!—It's a disgrace!

He's compromising the respectability of our town centre and the plan for suburban regeneration.

He's discrediting our Fatherland in the eyes of other Nations.

HE WON'T STEP IN LINE WITH EVERYONE ELSE TOWARDS THE ONE & ONLY GOAL OF THE

GREAT

MASTERWORK!

He's an outsider.

Negative. Ahistorical. Antisocial.

Unwholesome. He's corrupting the healthy local population.

An anarchist. Subverting order.

Disrupting the show

with the sound of his ocarina.

He stinks of cat urine.

—Several times he was stopped by the Immaculate Behaviour Police & kept overnight in jail where he was given the regulation shearing, but as soon as he was released in the morning he was seen breezing out the gate

of the Central Police Station, his hair grown back even curlier than before, as if nothing had happened.

!!!— He's an amoralist!

He infringes the Regulations.

He won't respect Authority.

He disqualifies the Institutions.

He rejects all discipline.

He's an unnatural, depraved individual.

A sado-oral pervert. How else to explain his fixation with constantly playing that dastardly ocarina.

He's a brute.

Louse-ridden.

Eccentric.

A sleazy type.

Polluting our good hard-studying smooth scented youth.

Insulting the virtuous baldness of our enlightened ruling class.

He won't go to church on Sundays.

He's an unbeliever

an atheist a heretic a ferment of dissolution

a germ from the filth of the unemployed bone-idle lumpen proletariat.

An excrement of the Nation.

Why don't we scour the city clean of such

vermin & abomination?!

—The city Authorities repeatedly enforced various special orders & confined him to house arrest in some

backwater

but each time they then issued a subsequent provision for urgent repatriation

since, following various plaints & complaints, one always came to the serious conclusion

that his confinement had actual damaging effects on the State budget

& the GNP.

The fact is

the technical-agricultural-industrial master workers of those peripheral locations

in their small-minded peasant-like provincialism

would neglect their tasks & obligations

to dance on the square around him as he played *Cielito Lindo* on his ocarina!

!!!! —Damnation!

He's a lowly minstrel of dumbed-down escapism.

He's a defeatist. He's a subversive propaganda man in disguise. An obsolete

traditionalist. A pseudo-engaged social climber.

An avant-garde buffoon. A maudit aesthete. An infected boil of

capitalist bourgeois decadence.

He diverts the faithful from Catechism.

HE IS STONEWALLING THE GREAT MASTERWORK!!

He promotes gatherings.

Incites the working class to strike.

Sabotages Football Matches & State

Tele-entertainment.

He's anti-progress. A Kafir. A mercenary agent provocateur. He must be taking orders from abroad.

He's at the service of the enemies of the people and of foreigners.

A self-styled street musician, but who's to say he's not a Castro guerrilla. A Soviet spy. One of Mao

Zedong's Red Guards. A sly killer in the pay of Judaic-American plutocracies.

He's a vulgar adventurer. A fanatic. A corrupted reactionary.

He eats soup with his hands.

He's a sold-out lackey of Capital. A most vulgar by-product of the industrial BOOM. A renegade

Trotskyite from the Sixth International.

He's a tax evader! He smokes other people's butt ends picked up from the pavement & smuggled marijuanas

LACKING the Imperial Stamp of the Monopoly on Tobacco Drugs etc.

He sleeps with the unlicensed whores of uptown commons

DEFRAUDING the Imperial Monopoly on Prostitution Tolerance etc., of the stamp duty.

He gets soused on the leftover juices of brandied berries

SWINDLING the Imperial Revenue out of the Extra Tax on Alcoholics Intoxicants etc.

He's a libertine. A drug addict. An alcoholic. A pimp.

He dishonours the Fatherland.

Outrages Public Morality.

Besmirches faultless Society. Desecrates the godliness of Families.

Vagrant of no fixed abode. Notoriously given to begging. Clearly drunk & disorderly.

What is

our efficient Police waiting for?

Sort him out!

—Alas! he has been repeatedly subjected to detention measures
as per Articles 27213-14-15 etc., of the Penal Code
but all the jails where he ended up soon begged for him to be transferred
judging him an UNDESIRABLE ELEMENT
until a final consolidated provision
decreed his PERPETUAL EXPULSION
FROM ALL THE PRISONS IN THE EMPIRE!

The responsible Chiefs have deemed him *frightful*—albeit, for a criminal, very peaceful.
He was always happy, giggly & well-mannered. Skipping around his cell like a gambolling lamb.
Sleeping on the bunk like on seven quilts, courteous even to bedbugs, that he addressed as 'signorinas'.
When lights-out was sounded, he always said 'Good night' to everyone, enjoyed the bread & cabbage
gruel like it was roast pullie

and as soon as anyone sneezed, he would say: *prosit.*

Yet

on account of his lamentable mental conformation he decidedly did not fit in with the penal institution

thus creating an intolerable

situation.

To begin with, he would confuse Guards with inmates and vice versa

citing the fact that the zebra-striped jackets

apt to distinguish criminals from the monochrome Guards

fatefully reproduced for him the optical-visual effect

of the authentic fauna of EQUINE ZEBRAS

towards which the Onager-Asses, his maternal grandparents

down there in his old native environment of Noah's Ark,

had inculcated

a special compulsory obsequiousness, as due to Sup., lordly and aristocratic

rank people.

So that

on the basis of such arch-damned coincidence said inmate would treat the base gang of

241 ~ THE WORLD SAVED BY KIDS

his joint jailhouse tenants with the most deferent Manner Codes of noble Good Upbringing

as if they were a Rotary Club Congress or a VIP banquet;

while addressing the Supervising

Personnel

in lenten strains of condolence & pity

as if they were poor devils serving a grim feudal majority!

Until (this perverse, malicious, illogical, crooked, gross & deadly

misunderstanding persisting)

all present went white-eyed and started boxing themselves on the head

deeming the universe totally topsy-turvy!!

It is our unfortunate duty to also report

the case of Guards seized by hallucinatory snobbery who started running as if possessed up and down the

cell block aisle announcing the daily bread & cabbage porridge IN THE FRENCH LANGUAGE and repeatedly

banging the keys on a slop pail or other ordinary vessel

in the belief it was a GONG!

and of other Guards who in a sudden frenzy of fanatic zeal set about

polishing the foot chains of common inmates, who meanwhile sat in lordly ease smoking a slim

'Van der Prinz Mercator'!

Anyone can see from such examples to what extent the presence of the above-mentioned inmate was

compromising the normal running of the Penal Institution.

One day, he made the ultimate blunder:

accosting the Chief Supervisor, he whispered confidentially

that he felt sorry for his misfortune, but was ready, if necessary, to teach him a practical & foolproof

means of escape, as easy to use

as any corkscrew or can opener!

!!!!!—Damnation!

He's made himself liable for nothing less than attempted bribery

of a civil servant in his full professional capacity.

He has a criminal record. Reoffending. Special watch unit. Habitual miscreant.

His cerebral malformation
jeopardizes the judiciary & legislative power
and threatens to unhinge the very structure
of the Imperial State.
He's a brain-damaged criminal!
with the precedent of apocryphal
ancestry
and the aggravating factor of street-performing
vagrancy.
He's a hereditary
chronic moronic!
TOTALLY DEVOID OF THE FACULTY TO APPREHEND THE IDEAL AFFIRMATION
& SOCIALLY SIGNIFICANT IMPLICATIONS

OF THE GREAT MASTERWORK!!!

Why can't we find a final solution
& intern him in some adequate institution?

—Hélas!

He had been interned, a while ago,
in the Imperial Psychotherapeutic Asylum
where all forms of mental disturbance
are cured by specialized personnel.

In fact, over there,
the inmates welcomed him at the entrance
with loud insistent acclamations
as if he were a superstar!

But soon enough
alas he stirred up a pandemonium
within the walls of the above-mentioned
sanatorium!

He would obstruct the therapeutic treatment
of patients, solicitously rushing over
to loosen the straps of their straitjackets.

Undergoing the same cure,
he displayed an abnormal ticklishness
with such associated episodes of extraordinary hilarity
as to cause his straitjacket to thunderously burst open
like an over-inflated balloon!

Treated with the cataleptic-hypnotic system
he proved resistant to all apt chemicals, barely achieving a sort of light ataxic nap
characterized by multiple ultra-resounding yawning, irrefutably displaying all the signs of BRAYING!
Whereupon, from all the neighbouring fields, and, echo by echo, beyond the outer borders
of our and our neighbouring
Empires,

each and every ass donkey & mule would wiggle their ears, forgetting their yokes, windlasses & carts
to send out in reply
thousands of tearing, fraternal, hysterical brayings.

Left awake, and placed (as per the basic
prophylactic criterion) in a cage,
he would immediately identify with a finch or canary, begin to flutter about & sing without respite
seized by a form of *contagious ornithomania*
whose germ would indiscriminately attack each & everyone around, be they doctors, nurses or patients.
So that similarly beset by coercive euphoria
singing & flying in flocks about the Psychotherapeutic Asylum
those wretches had reduced the austere Imperial State Infirmary
to an aviary!

To cut a long story short,
any therapy, when applied to this subject,

could only obtain the paradoxical effect
of worsening the manic outbursts of his sickness.
In view of which fact
the above-mentioned individual was fast-tracked
out of said Hospital
with the following certificate:

IMPERIAL STATE PSYCHOTHERAPEUTIC ASYLUM

RE.: PATIENT *unidentifiable*

RECORD NO. _____ *file not found*

WARD _____ *unclassifiable*

date—— (*unreadable*)

PERSONAL DETAILS: *Unqualifiable individual*
(Confidential information:
in light of sciencefictional investigation:
this seems to be the aberrant outcome of meteoric-alluvial fecundation
on an unreasoning animal subject),
suffering from a condition outside all norm
in virulent epidemic atypical untreatable form.

DIAGNOSIS: *undiagnosable.*
PROGNOSIS: *unprognosable.*

    MORAL: *Given the extraordinary combination*
and consequent unprecedented situation
the subject in question
is not dumpable on our competence
In faith & conscience
and in the official presence of State witnesses

SIGNED: *The Head of the Imperial Madhouse.*

—By a thousand devils!
Is the problem insoluble then?!
How is it possible that our advanced society
cannot come up with some sort of foolproof remedy
to free us from this trouble?!
He's a haven for germs!
A threat to public health!
Decimating our population!
Depleting the national zoo-technical stock!
JEOPARDIZING 'IN IPSO CORPORE' OF THE LOCAL AUDITORIUM
     THE TOTAL SUCCESS OF THE GREAT MASTERWORK!!!!
          Oh this is too much

               too much

!!!!!!

it's
TOO MUCH!

. . . .

Finally
recently
following the New Social Reform
a modern rational
solution
as regards the individual in question
was found at long last by scientific
elimination
via the pressure chamber.
Which is so called
because it consists of a vacuum-sealed room

pressurized & depressurized
by means of a piston on the outside.
Outwardly reminding one of a four-stroke
engine, it is known in hoodlum jargon as 'the dovecote'
because of its oblong whitewashed shape,
while the elegant language of the higher spheres
defines it as 'the room of atmospheres'.
Here, after a sojourn of variable duration
as per the authorities' specification,
the deviant individual
is—promptly or gradually—
eliminated.

   And so
the 'Pazzariello' affair
has finally been liquidated.

But before putting a full stop after this exemplary conclusion

it will not go amiss to make it clear

that prior to resorting to such a radical provision

one had tried all other possible means of integrating

the above-mentioned Pazzariello

so as to render him into an actively cooperating

member of the social organism of the New Empire.

In the first instance

(following a proposal from the New Higher Centre for the Advancement of Human Science)

he had been interned in the Neuropsychobiological State Institute

where the manic, the obsessed & the generally demented

are put to use and variously experimented upon

in the interest of the normal community.

But despite willingly adapting

to all sorts of high-risk procedures
—from major surgery carried out on a conscious subject
to autopsy carried out on a live individual—
he proved a subject of scarce scientific value
because practically
treatment-proof.
In the course of the above-mentioned works, at most he would
start huffing or sighing
from the boredom of lying
still for days on end on a dissecting table;
or while the time away by whistling *Cielito Lindo*
in his impatience to get back to his ocarina.
Now and then, out of good manners, he feigned interest in the work,
asking the surgeons: 'Everything all right?' or 'How's it going?'

or casting a semi-curious glance

at his own innards spread out on the table

and smiling good-naturedly as he

remarked: 'Blimey! Is all that stuff mine then?'

Then, when they untied him, he would unceremoniously start stretching

like a cat;

and no sooner had they stitched him back together than he jumped down happy & healthy,

saying 'Can I go now?'

The Medics, the Consultants & the Management were all agreed in declaring

his presence at the Neuropsychobiological State Institute

most inopportune.

He was meddling with the inmates' minds.

Compromising the seriousness of scientific traditions.

Whereupon, unanimously, at a plenary sitting, they ordered

his discharge.

And so, as per usual, after a brief absence, here he is again,

roaming the streets & cheerfully nodding to all his acquaintances

clearly convinced he must have been sorely missed

and that the whole population is happy & pleased to see him back so soon,

playing *Cielito Lindo* on his ocarina!

Until (thanks to the paternal interest

of the National Association of Productive Papas)

his case was taken up by the New Centre for the Rehabilitation of Deviant Minors

where, after the regulation head shaving,

he was assigned to a labour camp

with the job of making anti-tank mines, bombs & panzer nuts & bolts.

Note that said bunker-style labour camp,

made of solid cast iron charged with high-tension electricity & guarded by over 200 watchmen armed with machine guns,

is a supercamp, fully equipped to withstand any picaresque fancy stuff from the rehabilitees!

But after about half a week, nobody knows how, he

managed to escape

(one suspects that, eluding all vigilance,

he dug a passage out at night

with the help of some mine he had manufactured)

and here he is, back in circulation, with his curls grown fully back

walking around playing

Cielito Lindo.

With the nuts & bolts he had manufactured (a clear case of misappropriation)

and the residue of a neon tube

added to a tin of preserved foodstuffs

he had fashioned a sort of makeshift whistle

to use as a replacement for the confiscated ocarina.

He would point out that this was actually a trumpet;
but, one way or another, it sounded much louder
than the previous ocarina.

 It was unbearable!
A continuous provocation.
Now and then, at night, from far out at sea
one could hear explosions.
Notoriously, it was him
having fun with the bombs he had manufactured
as if it was midnight on New Year's Eve.
It's possible he was sending signals to the other shore
where some Bolivian or Congolese rebel might be lurking!
or even broadcasting to some foreign
reactionary radio station

a clandestine serialized novel with blasphemous criticism of our Social Reform!

People were sending letters to the papers:

Sir: how come we are still tolerating

this shabby individual freely circulating?

He was a notorious jailbreaking runaway.

In breach of the peace.

He had made himself responsible

for unlawful appropriation of State property

defence materials.

He was liable

for infringing the ban on the use of petards & explosives in general.

He was obstructing car traffic

with the sound of that pseudo-ocarina

that people mistook for a car horn.

He was defacing monuments!

A cleaning lady at the Museum of Race

looking down from a top-floor balcony

had seen him in the Monumental Park

exposing his most indecent parts

as he defecated behind a shrub.

He was offending modesty!

He was an invert!! And on top

of it all

the same cleaner, on the same occasion, had also

noticed that his indecent posterior parts

were small and muscular, Negro-type like.

Perhaps he was the bastard son of some mulatto.

In fact

his features did seem to show a certain prognathism.

He must have had at least a quarter African blood.

However,

those curls, that forehead—he had something of the Jew in him . . .

He must have had at least a quarter Jewish blood.

The daily *Above Board*, official information body of the New Empire,

published his photos front & profile

to exhibit his physiognomic defects.

The same paper's *Readers' Corner*

printed daily letters of concern on the Pazzariello case

from patriots, housewives & breadwinners.

People of sound judgement & sane mind

were all wondering what the use was of keeping this guy

—an idiotic illiterate half-breed

good for nothing but merry-go-lucking in the street

and living off the productive population.

An example of filthy, debauched, immoral living.
An outrage to our sober intellectual class, our wholesome college youth & our working people.
GIVEN TO SYSTEMATIC BOYCOTTING OF THE GREAT MASTERWORK!!!!!
An enemy of the Emperor, of the Proletariat, of the Race & of the Nation!
Following a provision from the Superior Authority
he was fast-tracked to pressure chamber
elimination.
Very good!
Very good!!

His curls
have become a pincushion
for Mrs Imperial Prefect, Exemplary Lady & Dame
who on top of all her various official accolades
(she is among other things the author of a delicate volume of verse

on family holidays

and founder of the benevolent *Fondlings' Shelter* for lost children)

devotes a part of her spare time

to fashioning bibs for the use of the National Crèche

on which she needlepoints stately mottoes praising the triumph of the New Empire

to edify the low-born newborns

and serve as MEMENTOES

for unlicensed whores & heartless mothers.

His skin

became a parchment-style griefcase

where the Prefect keeps the list of names of all Imperial Prefects and Police Chiefs

with relative dates of birth:

a useful MEMORANDUM

for H.E. the Prefect lest H.E. should fail to send those excellent servants of the New Empire

his timely personal wishes on occasion
of their birthdays and name days:
thereby sweetening with an exquisitely human touch
his and their onerous tasks
of high civil responsibility.

    And so

like it or not the Pazzariello
is now usefully serving the Imperial State
through its high representatives.
The Official Radio has broadcast the news
with the following comment:

    'It is the sacrosanct duty and right of every individual
    to fit into the perfect body of the State
    outside of which the human person is reduced

to an unqualified and superfluous cipher.
This and no other must certainly be
the occult significance
of the GREAT MASTERWORK travelling across our Empire during these days!
And so, let us address our deferent applause to our Emperor
who in his total clairvoyance allows
even the incapacitated and mentally defective
to employ their body, if unable to give their spirit,
in the service of cultural and civil Progress
and the ever more glorious events of the G R E A T
M A S T E R W O R K !!!!!!!!!'

But on our part, for the record, we have to report, as a final item about
said Pazzariello,
that the whole category of inmates

of the Neuropsychobiological State Institute
unanimously states to once have heard him say:
'that he set no store whatever by his body
which was a common object for temporary use
mainly serving, for the moment, his purpose
of roaming around playing *Cielito Lindo* on his ocarina.
Once used up, this object no longer concerned him
he would discard it like trash & garbage
skins & curls & all
and if people were so keen on picking up his garbage
they could make any shit they liked out of it.
Because he could easily get new bodies,
even much prettier bodies, whenever he fancied,
at no expense,
they being very easily manufactured objects.'

That's what
he had said
(for what mad people's statements are worth anyway),
adding as well
that these & other similar things can be read
and confirmed
in the famous scriptures of Buddha the Indian savant
of Christ the Galilean master
and of Socrates the Athenian philosopher

. . . .

And now—having closed the Pazzariello
parenthesis—
we are finally able to return to the main event
in today's programme: *The caravan*

of the Great Masterwork is in town . . . etc., etc.

Where were we? Oh yes:

' . . . the show unfolds among deafening comments . . . '

etc., etc., etc., etc. . . . Thus: as

a conclusion to all conclusions, no matter how much one discusses or reasons

or preaches or screeches—isolated, in a group, or in a crowd—

one cannot reach any plausible explanation

as to the actual significance of the Great Masterwork.

What one can see on one side contradicts & refutes

what is visible at the same time on the opposite side.

And whenever scholars patiently set to work

combining the several accounts into a whole,

arranging them in order like the fragments of a code

or the episodes of a serialized novel,

the end result is invariably

nothing but a haphazard & badly tangled mix

full of padding, useless repetitions, inconceivable oversights,

dead who come back forgetting they were dead,

tearings, swellings, suppurations, blanks;

an absurd, crippled, disconnected, disjointed text,

neither philosophical nor scientific or educational nor pleasant or pornographic or edifying nor reactionary

or revolutionary

neither comedy nor tragedy neither parody nor farce

devoid of common sense and Moral

with no head or tail.

It is nonetheless dutiful to recognize that the public is undeterred

and won't give up on the idea of making sense of it one day.

Among all the spectators the most optimistic

is always the type of the historian reporter
who braves a risky demanding manoeuvre
changing his place as the show progresses
along the entire perimeter of the scene
so that he can see all sides in sequence.
But—even assuming such circumambulation
might be accomplished in the short time of the show
and that he might come unscathed to the end of his endeavour—
he will have done so
to no avail.
For, while he was observing the effects on this side—or that—he was missing the contemporaneous effects
on that side—or this:
so that, in the end, he finds himself again & again with the same
common result.

The outcome is always as usual, the rule is general:
when the contraptions stop & the wings fold back down
into the switched-off caravan,
the theatre drama of the Great Masterwork has been understood
by none.

The only way to, MAYBE, get some inkling
could be to view all sides at the same time.
But only a freak growing to abnormal height,
in monstrous irredeemable illegality, finally doomed
to personally making himself invisible,
might manage to view all sides of the Great Masterwork
at once . . . .
    . . . and yet . . . .

. . . And yet in practice, such an extraordinary

adventure

would not at all change the normal

common result.

Indeed even if he came back

and gave the entire audience news of his discoveries,

who would listen?! in fact, who would forgive him?!

Our reporters have just informed us

that during today's performance of the Great Masterwork

(the one that's going on as we speak)

a four-month babe

was lynched by the enraged crowd

because, at a crucial point in the show,

with the audience in turmoil, he jumped out of his mother's arms and started flying in the air all around the stage wings,

shouting down to the audience, in all directions and

at the top of his lungs:

'LISTEN! Mum, Dad, brothers, sisters, Nanny, and the whole of my family! Friends and relations, people!!!

For goodness' sake, listen!! Why are you wrecking things like this?!

Calm yourselves, for goodness' sake! Let's all go back home!

WHY do you damn yourselves so?!?! . . . ALL OF THIS . . . how can you not realize?! . . . Listen to me, I'm

telling you:

ALL OF THIS

IN TRUTH AND SUBSTANCE

IS NOTHING

BUT A GAME.

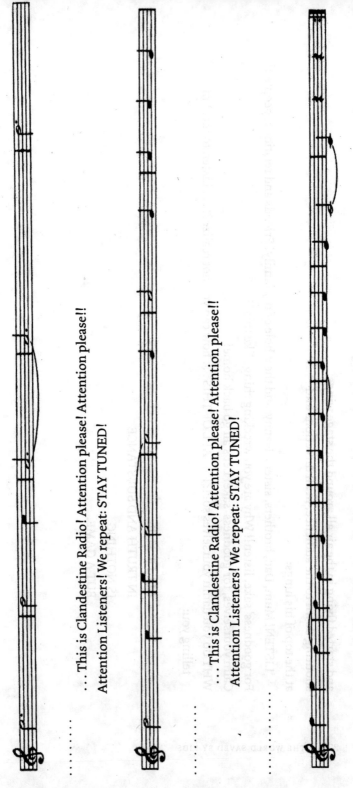

... This is Clandestine Radio! Attention please! Attention please!!
Attention Listeners! We repeat: STAY TUNED!

... This is Clandestine Radio! Attention please! Attention please!!
Attention Listeners! We repeat: STAY TUNED!

... This is Clandestine Radio! Attention please! ATTENTION PLEASE!

Attention Listeners! The programme resumes!

. . . .

. . . . ATTENTION PLEASE! Here we go! In today's programme,
your Sunday morning broadcast, we bring you an EXCEPTIONAL report:

At this precise moment, with special caring & acrobatic daring
we have succeeded in planting our clandestine microphone inside a canary's cage
overlooking the centre of the Imperial Square where the theatre Show is fully on the go!
!!!!!!!!

As you can tell from the blast of noise, the present run is deadly good fun!
Everyone's marching
      pushing & shoving

hairpulling
   slapping
      biting
             raping
beating
         fainting
screaming moaning laughing screeching huffing slamming falling rolling.
From what they say
it seems the fault is all
the poor's.
Hence as we speak the Sovereign has issued an OFFICIAL DECREE
mandating the COMPULSORY & RADICAL persecution
of the POOR! *Each and every one of the poor*
who within ten minutes (local time)
should have failed to prove

possession of a fortune equal to
a minimum of four hundred
thousand gold sterling deposited at the National Bank
will ipso facto receive the last rites and be moved to the Parish Morgue.

Radio hams, we urgently stress
that we are indisputably witnessing
global world history in the making:
an unprecedented slaughter taking place. Will you listen
to the screams the laments the baton blows the round-ups the hoorays the troubles the jaculatory prayers,
                                                                              drummings

& tocsin & diggings.
   Yet we are having to immediately advise you
that these hasty reports are already being superseded by the frantic pace of events. As we report, the
                                                                              self-propelled machinery

of the Great Masterwork continues to revolve

and right now it seems to have been ascertained that the main fault lies

with the

rich. A new Imperial Edict

was posted around the Square, proclaiming the enforcing of martial law

against the RICH!

Each and every one of the rich who within seven minutes (local time)

should have failed to show proof of proper have-not status

and to produce upon an officer's request

a police record immaculate of all profit and any personal effects

(except possibly for the prescribed one pillow and mattress)

will be immediately transferred to the Irregular Court

and sentenced to finance

his or her own

immediate

funeral.

Dear radio hams!! we cannot control our heartfelt emotion!!

ATTENTION PLEASE! ATTENTION PLEASE!! You have the chance, at this very moment, to tune in &

rejoice in being part of

the R E V O L U T I O N ! ! !

!!! Will you listen

to the banners clacking!

the powder stores cracking!

the high spheres' fall!

the ghostly roundabout in the dance halls!!!!

and the guitars the drums the catherine wheels the amnesties & venting of energies!! ! !! ! !

with the end of dynasties tyrannies raids mistreatings artilleries idolatries & hypocrisies!

And

the advent of poetries fantasies sympathies & authentic companies!! ! !! ! !

MAMMA MIA WE MADE IT! LONG LIVE OUR BEAUTIFUL SQUARE! But still the Great Masterwork keeps revolving. Will you listen

???

to the solid crowd talking in a contrite low voice, white-faced and lenten-lorn . . .

????

?????

???

?

. . . IN ORDER TO PROTECT THE REVOLUTION

FROM THE OBSCURE PROMOTERS OF REACTION

THEY HAVE ENTRUSTED IT TO THE PROTECTION

OF HIS MAJESTY THE EMPEROR, CLEAR MIRROR OF THE PEOPLE'S WILL.

!?

The crowd has stopped frolicking. And the Great Masterwork keeps revolving with a phenomenally obsessive effect.

Everyone has a black tongue & green complexion
worse than under a cholera infection.
Some throw themselves into the canal
some hang themselves from lamp posts.
And there are unconfirmed rumours that some newborn little critters
having cast a glance at the surrounding situation
have strangled themselves on the spot with their own umbilical cords!
A new Imperial Order has been printed:

It is the absolute will of the Sovereign to identify
the devious agents of reaction, responsible for all evil.
it is time to disclose to the public
a time-honoured, sacrosanct and undisputed
truth:
the fault lies entirely with
FEMALES OF FORTY AND OVER!

From the square comes a formidable ovation:
His Imperial Majesty is always right!
Enough sentimental piety!
Females over forty—who needs them?!
There & then a super-urgent regulation
is approved by acclamation:
In the name of the Revolution
and of the imperial people
all females throughout the nation
who are over the prescribed legal age
will be loaded post-haste onto a van
and heaped up at the State Crematorium!

Will you listen—attention radio hams,

can you hear the people's satisfaction now being voiced in loud chants

as mothers, spinsters, widows, grandmas great grandmas & aunts

all blaze up in a protean mass!

But the Great Masterwork has not stopped its revolving.

Here comes the crowd again, seething

worse than if they'd been seized by bubonic & pulmonary plague.

Not even the old-woman hunt has dissolved the nightmare of ages.

This infernal charade is still unresolved.

The culprits must be flushed out once and for all!

The guards of His Majesty the Emperor have just

posted a new notice on the wall:

May the struggle be relentless, categorical and systematic!

GET 'EM!!!! The worstest murderers, traitors of the Fatherland,

always were found among

singing volatiles
purloiners of birdseed
and especially CANARIES
because they're the colour yellow!

!

?.

..............??????????????........?

?.

?

?

?.

?

?

....

?..............

. . . . ?

? . . . .

! . . . This is

Clandestine Radio . . .

. . . Radio hams, you have just heard

the latest imperial proclamation!

We cannot deny that the situation

is getting critical and complicated.

This is no time to underestimate   the immediate danger of our position . . .

considering that we've chosen a canary's cage

as our microphone's

undercover location.

And meanwhile the criminal little twerp
won't stop its natural, carefree *chirp*!!!
You little wretch, can't you see
the X hour is coming for us?!
'Chirpy-cheep chirpy-cheep chirpy-cheep chirpy-chirp-cheep chirpy-chirp-cheep!'
Shush! Shush shush shush!
Shhshhss shh shhhhhh! shh . . .
phew . . . luckily that tiny little sound
was drowned out in a

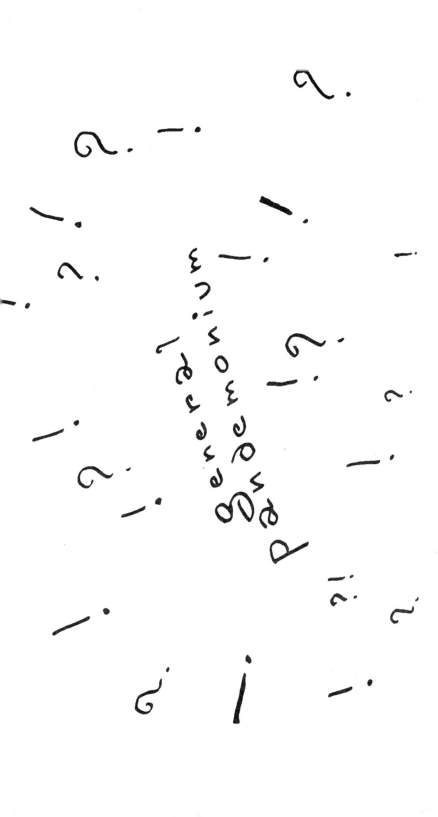

?! What's up now?! ATTENTION PLEASE! ATTENTION PLEASE !
STAY TUNED!

We are bringing you some EXCEPTIONAL news:

the Great Masterwork HAS STOPPED SPINNING!

it's listing! it's rolling!
the wings are rattling as if caught in a storm!
The whole auditorium is bamboozled
stock still in a breathless block
staring at the caravan!

ATTENTION PLEASE!

ATTENTION PLEASE!!!

STAY BY YOUR SETS!

Please synchronize your watches with the central timer at the Station:
it is twenty-four minutes to twelve...

...ATTENTION PLEASE! ATTENTION PLEEEEEASE! At this precise minute
we are reporting real time live

SENSATIONAL NEWS:

The Great Masterwork HAS SPOKEN!

and it's still speaking! What's it saying? W H A T's it saying??

Just now a a graduate polyglot
Swiss interpreter has arrived on the scene.
. . . but from what we can gather the Great Masterwork's voice
is fainter than a cricket's screech. . . .
Whatever it's saying, no one can hear a thing!

In the square the tension is reaching its peak:
from all sides the crowd is screaming: SPEAK! SPEAK!

. . . now they're rigging up a gigantic double loudspeaker . . .

. . . but unfortunately the awful din means we can't
pick up anything but scraps of gossip! . . .

......some say it's speaking some strange
    barbaric dialect no one can understand......
    ......some others say it's just repeating (respectfully speaking)
        just the one UNSPEAKABLE expression......

but we figure both versions must be utterly unreliable!
Do you think it's reasonable or admissible
for the G.M. to break its millenary silence
to spew forth obscene or senseless syllables?

....

ATTENTION PLEASE! ATTENTION PLEASE!

............ATTENTION PLEASE! ATTENTION PLEASE!

By means of an invisible high-tension cable, at this very moment we are able

to establish a live connection

with the giant loudspeaker standing by the contraption!

Here we go!

Perfect!!

Well done!!!

STAY by your sets!

HERE WE GO!

HERE WE GO!

HERE WE GO!

YOU ARE ACTUALLY LISTENING WITH YOUR VERY OWN EARS

to the

ACTUAL VOICE

of the

GREAT MASTERWORK:

'owooooo

owoooo owoo

owooooo owoo owoo owoo owoooo

xuiph

rhrrrrrrrrrrruikkkkk

.........trrrrrrrrrrrrrrrrrbr uhhhhhhhhhrumpf

xuiph xuiph xuiph

hhhhhhuigrrr

xuiph

aughaughaughaughaughauGHAUGHAUGHAUGHAU

GHAU ffvvvvvv

f vv

brrrrrhorrrrrr

owoo brrhorrrr brrrrrhooooobhooo

b...hh...hhh...hh...ooooooobBhoooooBHOOooooO....oOOOOMM!!!

hhhhhhhrrrrrruik

xuiph

!

?

??

RRRra . . . hams . . .

ATT
EN
t
ion

!

PL lee ee se !

You've   j . . .

heard

the bbbbbbbbbb

B . . . B . . . boom

of a huge exxxx explosion!

OHHHHHHHHH
Radio Hams this

is a

first !

The GRRR EAT MASTERWORK has gone & b bb

BURST!!!

(END OF BROADCAST)

At this final point, the clandestine radio set
(recoiling at the huge bang it had just broadcast)
started jumping and tottering
slowing down and leaning to one side
exactly like a top that's stopped spinning.
We could still hear
the faint notes of *Cielito Lindo*
fading away into outer space
among the last signals of the broadcasting station
going off.
And that was that. Today's programme
was finished.
Then she
picked up the set from the ground and stashed it like a
                                                    treasure
back inside the hem of her smock, sticking it back together
                                    perfectly well with saliva.
Then she looked up at the forest clock
—that was swaying from the ricochet of the distant bang
in the trees, all wavering like after a big gust of wind—
and said 'Blast! Nearly midday!
We better hurry up getting lunch together
otherwise, what with one thing and the other, we're going
    to be late
for the match!!!'
            But cool as a cucumber I
shot back:
'I've got a thousand liras!'
And straightaway
since she was goggling at my face,

looking none too convinced,
I pulled out that thousand note of mine, which was still
    creaking like it had just come out
of the factory.
  'A thousand!!!'
she shouted, gobsmacked like
she'd just seen a flying saucer,
'A thousand! printed! authentic! but then we're
awaaaaaay!!
Big time! we can go
to the deli, you know it's always open, Sundays too,
and eat the rice balls with mozzarella:
three, no, four each!
and after that we can buy two stand seats at the stadium:
forget the telly and the bar!!! and then,
after the match, we can go for pizza, you know the place,
                              near where the 29 stops
and eat one
supersize
each!!!'
  You can say what you like
but money is money
and always works with women, one way or the other.
As she spoke, she was looking at me in such a way that I felt
like when you open the window in the morning on a holiday
and hear the bells ringing.
And playfully she was twining her fingers with mine,
    exactly like the super-diva lovers do in the movies,
and laughing with surprise: and laughter made a little
    music in her throat
that gave me too a ticklish feeling in the throat

like when you play electric mandolin and don't know if
                    the music comes from you or the
                                        mandolin.
Seriously, I'm telling you again: you wouldn't dream of
    finding a girl this pretty,
not even if you're some financial tycoon!
For example: when she laughs, she
doesn't just laugh with her face, but with her little hands,
    her body, her feet!
not like tired old everyone else; more like certain animals,
                        who are better than saints
for friendship & company:
that lot, when they're happy, they laugh even with their ears,
and can't stand still,
so worked up they get!
And that's exactly the way
she laughed!
And at that moment, as her smock lifted, her
thighs came uncovered at the join, white and rosy, one
                        next to the other like two doves
with their nest of little black curls in the middle
shaped almost like a star . . .
That reminded me when I saw it of the whole night we'd
                        spent together
making love. And so at last
I had no more doubts, knowing
that she was really all mine, perhaps pregnant already.
And this thought made me laugh with happiness and trust,
because, when you start a family together,
the relationship is more solid.

Then in a happy rush I lifted her up by the arms, and we
both
felt like we were taking flight.
And together we ran off, skipping and dancing,
while she sang in time.
    Here are the words
of her little song:

> *Saltarello! rhumba! twist! samba! shake! and all the*
> *dances!*
> *Today is our wedding feast*
> *we laugh dance and sing without a care!*
> *Long live love, and long live kisses!*
>   *Saltarello*
>
>   etc.
>
> *Awake or asleep*
> *toad-ugly or hunks*
> *fifty years or one day*
> *hey*
> *what of that? . . . .*
> *ALL OF THIS, IN TRUTH AND SUBSTANCE*
> *IS NOTHING*
> *BUT A GAME.*

3

FINAL SONG OF THE YELLOW STAR
Also Called
the Charlottine

Here are my personal details
of the time when I was a young lass growing up in Berlin:
NAME, *Charlotte*.   PROFESSION, *Secondary school student*.
CITIZENSHIP, *Berliner*.   NATIONALITY, *Germanic*.
RACE,
Aryan.
   The dates I don't remember, because
I was never much good at History. And anyway, this is
                                      ancient history:
the fact dates back to the Twentieth Century.
The king of the Germans at that time was this guy Hitler,
and back then people went around saying
he was a HISTORICAL Fuehrer; but if I'm honest, to me he
                                      looked like
a threadbare little old man, with nothing special about him
except he was always screaming from the wireless.
Some said

he had another speciality: that his body was a prodigy of
                                        nature,
i.e. with no bones and no guts, made like a pneumatic sack,
so that he lived on air:
which would explain the derivation of that dubious word
    Aryan
that he threw among the subjects of the kingdom as
an honorific title.
But I can't say much at all
about certain paleozoological questions.

The whole world was aware
that our king was at that time preparing
a most glorious worldwide superwar.
Every single space was covered in photos of him,
but if I'm honest, for me
the more these were wasted by the thousand the less effect
                                        they had,
to the point I found them almost invisible,
as if they were adverts against hair loss.
I had other fish to fry,
at fourteen! Now that *that* Charlotte is no more, I can talk
                                        about her
as if she were someone else . . . I was in my early adolescence,
not too tall but not short either, with rounded knees
and dimples at my elbows,
and when I laughed, everyone laughed!
At school, among my friends, my nickname was:
die goldlottchen, i.e. *the little golden Charlotte*,
because I had little golden curls, and golden eyes too,
and a sprinkle of golden

freckles
on my arms and high on my cheeks.

On one of those days, in the month of April,
every street in Berlin showed on its walls
an Important Notice, headed by the royal crest
(which was like a skew-whiffed double hook)
and underneath, the following
Order:

ACHTUNG!
ARYANS! PEOPLE OF THE GREAT REICH!
In the name of our great FUEHRER
and of all ministers, undersecretaries, ss.,s.a.s, servicemen
and underservicemen of the great REICH
and of all the generals officers underofficers and troops
of the glorious army of the great REICH
and of all the HIERARCHIES of the Great Nazi Party down to
grade K .
WE HEREBY ORDER
That by the end of tomorrow each and every individual of
non-Aryan i.e. Judaic race
shall provide him or herself with the regulation yellow star
to be visibly worn & displayed as a compulsory badge.
Any Jew
caught circulating within the town of Berlin or anywhere
within the territory of the great REICH without
the above-mentioned badge
shall be immediately brought before the special Tribunals
that act day and night without interruption.
CITIZENS! PEOPLE ALL OF THE GREAT ARYAN REICH!

For the sacrosanct purpose of safeguarding the pure Aryan blood
from the filthy Judaic contagion
we are counting on your iron-willed vigilance so that
any attempted disobedience of the present order
on the part of the Jews
is immediately
nipped in the bud.
LONG LIVE OUR GREAT REICH! LONG LIVE OUR GREAT
FUEHRER!
LONG LIVE OUR GLORIOUS ARYAN RACE!

Since people were stopping in front of this notice,
I'd got curious; but reading it, I was perplexed:
to me, there was something not quite right with it.
Namely: the Jews' DISOBEDIENCE
was expected—not so the Aryans'. On the face of it,
it seemed that, for the Aryans (whatever
this obscure title might mean anyway), disobedience
would be a case wholly negating logic,
like a cat starting to fly.
For me, the notice was wrong. I felt an itchy little tickling in
     my shoulder blades,
which for me is the first sign of wanting to laugh:
and there and then, suddenly, an attack of fun persuaded me
to transform that ordinary obedience into an
extraordinary
disobedience.
The next morning, I proudly stepped out on the streets
with the Jews' yellow star
shining on my chest like a rose.

Certain attacks of fun are just like musical notes
that cannot live alone: instinctively a note will join another
in a chord; and a chord calls for another and another, and
                                    they go into the theme;
and the development; and the refrain.
And from the allegro you go to the andante maestoso; and
    to the presto; and to the final prestissimo!
And so, the season's amusement was born.
The first Aryans to imitate me right away were
the naughtier schoolfriends, the whimsical girl friends.
Other fresh-faced students from all classes are following
                                    them: already some of the teachers
are feeling a tingle of imitation . . .
Little clandestine forgers
are at work fashioning Judaic stars.
In four or five days, students
are joined by bar boys, bakery boys, young labourers,
and then soldiers, sailors, Herr and Von,
dames, waitresses and prostitutes
priests and friars and nuns.
Everyone is sporting the yellow star
the stars are multiplying by the thousand
the yellow star is all the rage!
Any clothes look almost like mourning wear
without that brazen, fascinating star!
Ach! screams the Gauleiter,
the Municipal Archives didn't show
so many Jews living in Berlin!
More than half the population is Jewish?!?
Ach! Ach!! ACH!!! But by the time

the Authorities'suspicion
takes the shape of an investigation,
it's too late already.
(Of course: because if the Authorities were more intelligent
they wouldn't put up with the extreme ridiculousness
of authoriting!)
ACH!!! Can't make head or tail of it!
Almost the whole population is Jewish?!?
Too late, Mr Gauleiter. Too late, Fuehrer.
By now, the whole Authority corps can go fuck themselves.
As soon as some police mug shows up
it gets surrounded by a chorus of starry kids
who skip and jump around him singing the latest hit:
Jude Jude will you marry me
don't keep me sighing sad and blue
Aryan as I may be
I've got my gold star too'.
Strange phenomena begin to occur:
for instance, the police force itself
surrounded by the chorus, has been known to fall into a
    hypnotic state
and bamboozedly start singing
Gold Star.
And finally the inevitable miracle explodes!
One morning, in the space of an instant
those myriads of yellow stars all together
are seen to turn into authentic solid gold!
The crowded Unter den Linden looks like a firmament
in broad daylight!
And from the deep, fine dust of the sky there comes

a flight of birds—or that's what it looked like from afar—
   Is it starlings? swallows?
storks? ... Well ... no ... NOOO!
It's the angelic hosts! in full order!
Angels, Archangels and Principalities,
Powers, Virtues and Dominions,
Thrones, Cherubim and Seraphim.
All boys (or girls?) of stupendous
and much varied beauty: next to a sunflower-
blond Archangel, his flesh the colours of sunrise on the sea,
is another Archangel of tawny Sicilian pallor, with a head of
                        curls like a little basket of black grapes.
A Pygmy of sublime cherubic grace
is racing in flight with a Chinese cherub
that looks like a bird of Paradise. A smiling Indian Throne
of regal stature is holding hands
with a little Semitic angel, a masterpiece
of a little statue sculpted in delicate ivory.
But perhaps the supreme beauty
is a Black Dominion, alone at the front of the host, testing out
his tenor saxophone made of red gold.
Each and everyone has a gold armour
double gold wings (the first two, huge, unfolded in the air,
the other two, of lesser size, folded over the abdomen, like
   two leaves
of a marvellous and comely plant)
and all carry trumpets and flutes and tubas and saxophones,
                                                      etc.,

all made of gold.
Gliding through the air

together in a circle they surround the Reichstag;
and the Black Dominion
blows first into his instrument
sounding the notes of a reveille
(*Wake up, wake up, Awkward Squad!*)
immediately followed by the entire orchestra
unleashed in unison.
The government building shudders
under the immense musical effect as at the passage
of twenty-five supersonic reactors
and almost simultaneously three windows on the upper floors
open to show
Hitler Adolf, known among kids by the nickname
    of Monotache or also Goffukk,
Goering Hermann, aka Fatso or Tripes,
and Goebbels Paul Joseph, nicknamed Jaundice.
Their three maniacal faces
are looking up, distorted by a horror so naked
as to look indecent.
Nothing is really more tragic
than madness
in its indecent forms: and to laugh at it would certainly be
    unfair. But angels are kids after all,
and in fact more full of fun, for being angels, than
    all possible kids
and seeing the alienated expression of those three characters,
like in front of a funny show, they give themselves up to
                                        indescribable hilarity
almost turning breathless with laughter and dancing
for more than half a minute, suspended up there in the sky.

Finally a certain quiet returns to those restless ranks.
And the Chinese cherub is pushed forward,
who speaking for the entire company
addresses those three fetish masks
in a feminine voice like a nightingale's:
'Why are you grimacing like madmen?
We have come only to tell you
that your war
is over
even before it began.
But you mustn't get too upset.
One day, in a long time for you (but not for us)
you too, you poor pimping, murdering devils
will inevitably have to
return
to Paradise.
And there on that day we will explain to you why
your war
yes that too
anyway it went, lost or victorious, and no matter how
   dismal, obscene and ferocious you might have made it
            ULTIMATELY
            IN TRUTH AND SUBSTANCE
            THAT TOO
            COULD ONLY EVER HAVE BEEN
            NOTHING BUT
            A GAME.'

Envoi

And now, you who have listened to these songs,
forgive me if I sigh thinking back
on how simple
my life had been.

NOTES

AUTHOR'S NOTES

The Evening at Colonus

Some of the broken and reiterated sentences spoken by the Chorus are taken from P. H. and death camp records, ancient and modern political speeches, etc. Other quotations scattered throughout the Chorus' lines or spoken by various characters come from ancient Aztec chants,[1] from Sophocles,[2] from an old chain-gang blues,[3] from the Hebrew Hymn for The Dead,[4] from the *Instructions For Recruits*,[5] from the Bible,[6] from the Vedas.[7]

1 Page 62: *In Tlatelolco | the fire turns black*; page 70: *Divine water blazing!*; page 90: *Will I ripen again into an ear of corn?*; page 90: *Will I seed myself . . . ?*

2 Page 100: *It's ready | this robe . . .* ; page 101: *It's ready! It's ready, this | mortuary robe . . .* ; page 106: *Here it comes again | the ferocious . . .* ; page 116: *And here I am again | here in the vice grip . . .*

3 Page 71: *Go down ole man . . .* (addressing the sun)

4 Page 86: *Yitgadal . . .*

5 Page 122: *Step in time . . .*

6 Page 123: *Give drink . . .*

7 Page 126: *Heaven and earth . . .*

The verses divided into syllables (*Ad-iter . . .*) on pages 127–8 come from the Rig Veda and mean: *Aditi begat Daksha—and Daksha begat Aditi.*

The verses in italics on pages 132–3 (*yes, yes . . .*) are by Allen Ginsberg [in E.M.'s translation].

The poem in inverted commas on page 133 (*O Sacred Being!* etc.) is by Hölderlin [in a free-rhythm translation by E.M].

The Yearning for Scandal

The verses or phrases quoted in French on pages 138, 145, 147 and 153 are by Rimbaud.

The phrase in German on page 142 is sung by Papageno in *The Magic Flute*.

The World Saved by Kids

On page 215, *al-jabr . . .* is Arabic for 'algebra'.

TRANSLATOR'S NOTES

In keeping with Morante's sense of the book as a work deeply
rooted in song and storytelling (her early drafts even bearing
plans for instructions on the singing of various parts), I have
tried to follow the original rhythm and rhyme pattern as
closely as possible: this has sometimes resulted in small
alterations to line breaks and other layout elements.

After much deliberation, I have localized the translation
on one or two occasions, where I felt that keeping too strictly
to the original regional references would be detrimental to
the consistency of tone required. Conversely, I have used a
variety of non-standard terms to give a sense of the 'broken
Italian' heavily inflected with Roman dialect spoken by
Antigone in *The Evening at Colonus*: hopefully that will carry,
especially when recited or even just read aloud, some of the
high tension achieved by the original.

I have re-translated the quotes from Tsvetaeva and
Hölderlin from the versions given by Morante in the origi-
nal, and chosen not to correct the slight inaccuracies in her
usage of German words (*cf* the quote from *The Magic Flute* on
page 142 and *Final Song of the Yellow Star* on page 304).

Although some of the terms used in the original
('negro', 'Eschimesi', 'cannibali Zulù') might for very good

reasons be frowned upon today, I felt that altering or suppressing them in the translation would have given an inaccurate picture of the times and context in which the book was written.

Page 29, *Late Sunday Dusk*

The title respects the acronym deliberately created by the original title, *La sera domenicale*.

Page 31, in the base body

From the formula *in corpore vili*, thought to be used by sixteenth-century physicians to justify experiments on the bodies of commoners.

Page 32, *peacock named Scheherazade*

In keeping with the theme of androgyny woven like a red thread through the text, Morante creates a *pavonessa*—not a peahen (*pavoncella*) but a mythical, if wounded, creature who has the colours of a fantastic male bird and the allure of the queen of stories.

Page 71, *Go down ole man*

Adapted by Morante from the original Texas prison-camp song 'Go Down Old Hannah'.

Page 111, *killer cool dude*

Morante here uses the word *mafioso* in its original sense (roughly meaning 'someone arrogantly beautiful and showily dressed').

Pages 122, 177, *alalà*

An ancient Greek war cry popularized and used in Italy during the years of the Fascist regime.

Page 148, QUANNO MAMMETA ...

From a Neapolitan folk song (*When your pretty mama made you | do you know what she put in | honey sugar cinnamon | honey sugar cinnamon*).

Page 149, Chiagneva sempre ...

From a Neapolitan song about the death of a beloved girl (*She always used to cry sleeping alone | but now sleeps in the company of the dead*).

Page 176, *Paolo Rossi*

A left-wing student whose death at La Sapienza University in April 1966 sparked massive occupations and the resignation of the rector.

Page 263, *griefcase*

Lifted (with thanks) from a poem by Peter Redgrove.

Page 310, Awkward Squad

The original term Morante uses here is a truncated form of the word *cappellone* ('big hat'): this was old Italian army slang for a goofy recruit—not to be confused with *capellone* (a long-haired fellow or hippy).